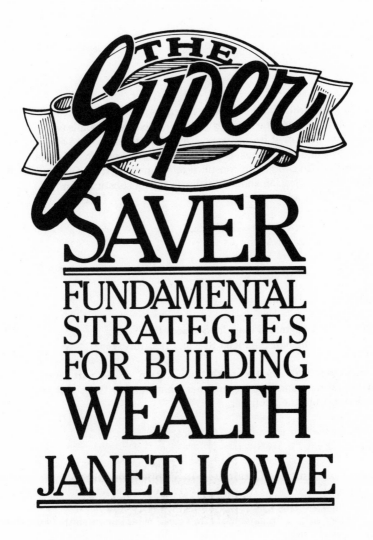

THE Super
SAVER
FUNDAMENTAL STRATEGIES FOR BUILDING WEALTH
JANET LOWE

Longman Financial Services Publishing
a division of Longman Financial Services Institute, Inc.

While a great deal of care has been taken to provide accurate and
current information, the ideas, suggestions, general principles and
conclusions presented in this book are subject to local, state and
federal laws and regulations, court cases and any revisions of same.
The reader is thus urged to consult legal counsel regarding any points
of law—this publication should not be used as a substitute for
competent legal advice.

Executive Editor: Kathleen A. Welton
Project Editor: Ellen Allen
Interior Design: Sara Shelton
Cover Design: Anthony Russo

© 1990 by Janet Lowe

Published by Longman Financial Services Publishing
a divison of Longman Financial Services Institute, Inc.

Printed in the United States of America.
90 91 92 10 9 8 7 6 5 4 3 2 1

Library of Congress Cataloging-in-Publication Data

Lowe, Janet.
    The super saver : fundamental strategies for building wealth / by
Janet Lowe.
        p.   cm.
    Includes bibliographical references.
    ISBN 0-88462-915-5
    1. Saving and thrift—United States.   I. Title.
HG7931.L67   1990   89-12646
332.024'01—dc20   CIP

Dedication

To my mother and father, David W. and Celesta A. Lowe, who taught me the value of many things, the most important of which is having loving parents.

Acknowledgments

I would like to express special appreciation for the contribution that many people made to this book.

In particular, thanks to Marilyn Cohen, Capital Insight Inc. of Beverly Hills, for her abundant information on government securities; Risé Husmann, for her advice on insurance matters; my husband, Austin Lynas for his patience and his careful reading of the manuscript; to Alice Martell, author's representative, for the speed and thoroughness of her work; Mary Smalligan, a partner at Deloitte, Haskins and Sells, for her counsel on tax matters; Kathy Welton, Longman Financial Services, a first-rate editor; Charlotte Wingfield, senior vice president of Imperial Corporation of America, for her excellent suggestions regarding financial institutions and accounts; and to Robert Witty, for being a supportive boss.

Though there are too many of you to name individually, my gratitude also goes to those who encouraged the writing of this book, and who gave me their moral support during its conception and development.

INTRODUCTION

"Poverty is no vice, but an inconvenience."

JOHN FLORIO, *Second Frutes*

When it comes to having fun, for most people, saving money rates right up there with being on a diet, going to the dentist or shampooing the carpet. There are times you just have to do these things, but . . .

Maybe Americans feel a little put off when they think about saving money because of the consumerist, service-oriented world in which we live. Quick gratification of whims, desires, and needs has become commonplace. We're used to having what we want right now, whether it's gourmet food, clothes, cars, or a caper on the beach in Hawaii.

But there is a reward for dieting—a slimmer figure and better health. You avoid pain and flash a brighter smile after visiting the dentist. And when you scrub the carpet you get a cleaner, lovelier home; you can be proud when friends come over.

THE REWARDS FOR SAVING ARE SENSATIONAL

There are rewards for saving money too—big rewards. It is a seeming paradox that when you save more money you have more money to spend on the people and things that make you happiest.

Perhaps the biggest rewards are intangible. Good savers:

- Are in charge of their own destiny
- Run their own daily lives
- Are free to take risks on the job. Enjoy enormous peace of mind.

Saving money on a regular basis once was a respected American habit. It was a virtue taught at home, at church, and in the schools. Children were encouraged to open bank accounts and deposit nickels, dimes, and quarters on a regular basis. Many changes, both in our society and in the system that delivers financial services, have conspired to alter our saving habits.

In fact, it is questionable whether Americans, who have the lowest savings rate among the major industrial countries and who are saving at the lowest rate in this nation's history, have any saving habits at all.

THE NEED FOR SAVING IS ENORMOUS

We may need to learn how to save again. Consider these facts:

- Because housing costs have escalated in many parts of the country, young people have begun to worry that they won't be able to afford to buy a home. What they may not realize is that cheap and easy-to-finance housing is a thing of the past. Following World War II, the nation turned its attention to building affordable homes for returning soldiers and their families. The average 30-year-old homeowner in the 1950s, reported *Changing Times* magazine, could make the monthly mortgage payment using 14 percent of pre-tax monthly pay. In 1971 it took 21 percent and in 1984, 44 percent.

- Financial experts believe it may be more difficult for the babyboom generation, the 76 million people born between 1946 and 1964, to fund its retirement dreams than it is for today's retirees. Why? Because there are so many of them vying for goods and services, because their vast numbers will place a heavy burden on the Social Security system, and finally, because many members of this consumer-oriented generation have more ambitious retirement plans.
- College costs are soaring. As federal and state governments look for places to cut spending so taxes can be trimmed, government grant and loan programs for students are likely to suffer. It will be increasingly difficult for young people to afford a higher education. It is estimated that by the year 2000, four years of education at an average public institution will cost close to $50,000. At a private university, the bill could be as high as $100,000, according to the College Board. Both students and their parents need to face facts early and establish a savings plan.

These are only a few of the reasons we need to learn more about saving and discover the least restrictive, most interesting and pleasurable ways to build a nest egg. Taking care of the nest and getting the eggs to hatch and grow is just as important a job for savers as it is for investors. *The Super Saver* was written to help Americans reach their dream of achieving greater economic security by saving more of what is earned.

WHAT IS SAVING?

Economists define personal saving as "not spending," or any part of personal income that is not consumed. That broad explanation probably works well for ivory-tower theorists, but in our personal lives, at home, it is necessary to be more precise.

To start with, *savings* and *investment* are not terms to be used interchangeably. Too often, they are seen as the same thing. "I put my life savings in an oil and gas limited partnership," the sorrowful widow might say. The sad fact is, once she put her money into such a risky venture, it became an investment. She no longer had any savings.

When a clear distinction is made between the two terms, the difference is easy to understand.

Investing Is Not Saving *Investing* implies taking a special kind of risk in order to reap a higher return. Capital, to be exact, is put at risk. If you buy stock in a company, there is a chance that you won't make a return on that investment. There is a further risk that your initial investment—the capital—will be lost. The share price of the stock could decline from the price at which you bought in, and it might never return.

This is not to imply, however, that investing is bad or wrong. At the correct time and in the appropriate way, it is exactly right.

Save with Serenity While there probably is no completely risk-free place to store money, *savings vehicles* will be defined as those instruments that promise the return of capital.

Being wise savers, we will want that capital back with interest earned—at the highest rate it is possible to arrange under the prevailing conditions. Savings accounts, certificates of deposits, corporate bonds, most annuities and treasury securities fall into this category. And there are other places to save as well.

Recognizing Risk As for the risks, all will be discussed, from the danger of the erosion by inflation, to the possibility of default on bonds, to the threat of collapse of a savings institution.

A HAPPY, HEALTHY ATTITUDE

There is one other point that readers should think seriously about and keep in mind while studying this book. A healthy attitude toward money is essential. Attaining wealth is both wholesome and wise. But money should not be viewed as a substitute for love, power, acceptance, entitlement, freedom or any other psychological need.

The real meaning of money, as Dr. Edward M. Hallowell and William J. Grace, Jr., point out in their book *What Are You Worth?*, is simply "a tool to help us live our lives in comfort."

A ROAD MAP FOR READERS

It will be helpful for readers to understand how the information in this book is organized and what lies ahead. *The Super Saver* is divided into four sections, each designed to build upon the next. A subject that may at first seem complex will become easy to understand as the chapters progress.

The initial section deals with establishing motivation for saving. What difference does it make to an individual, a family, a nation of people? The amazing possibilities of a saving plan will be contrasted with the dangers of debt, and then the message becomes clear. A saving plan makes a major difference to financial security.

The second section of this book focuses on how to save—figuring out how much a person should save, how to set goals, and how to allocate savings to the appropriate vehicle.

Section three lays the groundwork for choosing specific accounts. Interest rates, inflation, taxes, and their impact on savings practices will be covered. Furthermore, readers will discover how to do their own arithmetic when dealing with interest rates, compounding, taxes, and other financial questions.

In the fourth segment, the book gets down to the specific details of selecting a safe and convenient financial institution with which to work; picking a treasury security over a bond or a certificate of deposit or a money market fund; and finally, understanding the level of risk involved in most of the diverse money repositories that are available today— in short, detailed information on the possible places to store money.

After completing *The Super Saver*, the reader will be equipped to make conservative yet sophisticated decisions regarding the most fascinating and fundamental aspect of money management—saving.

And it is the author's hope that new savers will derive great pleasure from the control they now will have over their finances.

CONTENTS

tors? • Checking Credentials • FDIC Predominates • How Federal Insurance Functions • Multiple Accounts • IRAs on Their Own • Testing for Strength • Ask an Expert

PART
1

The
Importance
of
Saving

CHAPTER 1

Why Save?

*"To be poor and independent is very nearly an
impossibility."*

WILLIAM COBBETT, *Advice to Young Men*

A review of current books on personal finance revealed a
surprising circumstance. While they discussed home ownership, investing, retirement, and dozens of other important
aspects of financial planning, almost all of them ignored a
critical tool of financial management, the path that most
of us must walk before we are able to buy a home, play the
stock market or plan for those happy golden years: They
forgot about the first step—saving.

STEP ONE

Saving requires as much thought and strategy as other ele-
ments of a financial plan. "You can't live well by accident,"
wrote Theodore Miller, editor of *Changing Times* magazine,
in his book *Kiplinger's Make Your Money Grow.* "If there
ever was a time when you could achieve financial success
through fitful effort combined with a little good luck, that
time is long since past."

The question "Why save?" may seem simplistic and perhaps juvenile at first glance. Every adult knows it's a good thing to save. Even a lot of kids know that.

GOOD REASONS PROVIDE INSPIRATION

Nevertheless, not every adult is motivated to save. That fact is clear when one considers the shockingly low U.S. savings rate. To be motivated to save, each person must seriously think about why he or she should save. What is there to gain? What is there to lose? What difference would a savings plan make to his or her life?

As a result of one's thinking about why it is important to save, the motivation often presents itself naturally. Furthermore, savings goals point the way to the most appropriate savings method.

The many reasons to save fall generally into three major categories:

- For security
- For a specific purchase, such as a home, car, or holiday
- To earn income on which to live, to supplement employment income, or for retirement income

SAVING FOR SECURITY

"The motive of savers to avoid financial insecurity was the bastion of bank and savings and loan advertising of the 1950s and 1960s," according to Charlotte Wingfield, a senior vice president with Imperial Corporation of America, parent of San Diego-based Imperial Savings. "But this motive of 'saving for a rainy day' dropped sharply in the public's minds in the 1970s and 1980s. The increasing government provision of health, education and income security benefits has altered the objectives associated with savings for many people."

Wingfield wrote those words in the late 1980s when Americans were just beginning to suspect that some benefits they had counted on might not be there when they are needed. The government seemed to be spending Social Security reserve funds as fast as contributions were made. Corporate restructuring tempted companies more and more to tap into retirement plan reserves. Workers were being required to contribute more and more to their own health insurance plans. In fact, studies showed a disturbing statistic: In 1988, it was estimated that 37 million Americans had no health insurance at all. The trend toward hiring on a part-time basis only has cut off many U.S. workers from benefits their parents took for granted.

BANKRUPTCY REGISTER

The need for a return to financial security as motive for saving can also be demonstrated by the bankruptcy rate, which continued to rise even in the prosperous second half of the 1980s.

For the 12-month period ending June 30, 1988, there were 526,066 non-business bankruptcy filings, an 11 percent increase over the year before, according to the Consumer Credit Institute of the American Financial Services Association. Between 1983 and 1988, the number of Americans filing bankruptcy nearly doubled.

THE MENACE OF POVERTY

If the preceding discussion isn't frightening enough, consider these facts offered by *City & State* magazine in January 1989, a time when the country was enjoying the longest period of uninterrupted prosperity in its history: "Despite the continuing economic recovery, a major legacy left by President (Ronald) Reagan will be increasing hunger and homelessness in the nation's major cities, according to a report by the U.S. Conference of Mayors."

Mayors in 27 cities responded to a survey by the magazine which reported that "During the past year, requests for emergency shelter increased by an average of 13 percent across the survey cities." Pleas for emergency food assistance "increased in 88 percent of the responding cities, by an average of 19 percent," the story continued.

It is likely that many of the homeless and hungry represented in the study had always been poor and perhaps never had the opportunity to save. But the survey statistics also show that about 49 percent were single men, and 26 percent of those were veterans. At one point in their lives, while they were in military service at least, those men had an opportunity to save for the future.

Hindsight can be 20-20. But those reading this book have a chance to look ahead. Most people find a special comfort in having money stashed away in a safe place, quietly growing as inflation eats away at other provisions of their budget.

ANYONE CAN HAVE BAD LUCK

Those who have saved are less prone to be worried about an economic slump that may cut into commissions, bonuses, or pay raises. Though nobody likes the thought of losing a job, savers are less tortured over the possibility of being temporarily out of work. They can more easily go about their lives with self-confidence and a certain elan. In short, people who save to build a financial cushion also create peace of mind.

SAVING FOR A SPECIAL PURCHASE

Putting aside money for a future purpose has always made sense, since the more money a buyer initially puts into a home, car, or major appliance or toward a vacation, the lower payments are likely to be and the less total interest charges will be. (In Chapter 2, the high cost of borrowing will be investigated further.) But when the Tax Reform Act

5

of 1986 was passed, the incentive to save, rather than to use credit for current and intermediate-term purchases, was enhanced. The revised tax law disallowed the write-off of consumer interest.

Coming up with the standard 20 percent down payment on a home is one of the greatest incentives for saving in this country today. Because homes are more costly than they once were and it's taking young people longer than ever to accumulate that money, Congress in 1989 was considering a proposal to permit taxpayers to tap their Individual Retirement Accounts (IRAs) without penalty before age 59½ if the money is used for a down payment on a home. Unfortunately, many young people have not been able to establish an IRA either.

THE HAPPIEST HABIT

All in all, special-purpose saving, usually of three months' to five years' duration, is the type in which many savers find the most satisfaction. It is how they plan for Christmas spending, vacations, a new off-road motorbike, or a new car. The payoff can be quick and fun.

TEMPTATIONS OF BORROWING

For many people, however, it's easier to *finance* these types of purchases—to buy now and pay later. So the temptation to spend in advance, rather than save for intermediate-length goals or consumer durable goods, is greater. In fact, with longer-length loans available, some consumers find themselves continuing to pay for clothes, appliances, or vehicles that have long-since worn out.

While clever management of consumer debt offers the greatest opportunity for improvement of one's financial situation, it also is consumer debt that is most likely to lead to personal financial difficulty.

Even with greater motives and tax incentives to avoid credit card debt or consumer loans, consumer installment credit in 1988 increased 8.9 percent over 1987, according to statistics from the Federal Reserve Board. The ratio of household debt to disposable income rose from 49 percent in 1960 to 54 percent in 1970 to nearly 63 percent in 1980, according to Prudential-Bache economists. But that still wasn't the peak: In 1987, the ratio hit 74.3 percent, an all-time high.

There are some signs of improvement, however. The American Bankers Association reported that in 1988, 40 percent of credit card holders paid off their full balances each month, thus avoiding double-digit interest rate charges. That compares with 33 percent in 1987.

A SUBTLE REMINDER

To counteract promotions by retailers to encourage customers to charge more, one consumer group created a warning sticker for credit cards similar to those on cigarette packs. Called a "d-e-b-t-rimental warning," the self-stick label reads "WARNING: Overuse Can Be Dangerous to Your Wealth!"

SAVING FOR INCOME

Probably nobody is more sensitive to saving for income than older Americans, many of whom were able to earn interest rates of more than 20 percent on U.S. Treasury securities in the late 1970s and early 1980s. That was the heyday for savers. Unfortunately, they reaped their rich rewards at the expense of other taxpayers and consumers.

While the dazzling rates of the early 1980s are gone, the government and U.S. financial institutions have nevertheless been highly imaginative in creating securities and new types of deposit accounts that allow consumers to improve their income, while at the same time taking relatively little risk with capital.

This approach will be attractive, even essential, to many people, including:

- Retired people, or those nearing retirement. Savers in this category realize that once their principal (their fundamental hoard of savings) is lost, they will have more and more difficulty replacing it through work. Preserving capital becomes a high priority in the later years.
- Heirs of any age who receive a settlement from an estate. For many heirs, the inheritance will be a one-time event, and they will want to ensure that the gift increases their standard of living over a long period of time. Saving that money in fixed-income accounts is an ideal way to accomplish that goal.
- Recipients of insurance settlements, especially if the settlement is for an incident that has left a physical handicap. Again, a lump-sum settlement must be protected, and income from it must be maximized. Exceptional caution is warranted, because nobody presents a greater mark for perpetrators of fraud than someone who has recently collected on a large insurance claim. Scam artists have ways of discovering people who have received lump-sum payments, and they often are ruthless in their schemes to lure that money into their own pockets.

ENCROACHMENT OF INFLATION

Savers are particularly vulnerable to inflation. In fact, it was the high inflation era of 1978 to 1982 that spurred Americans on to record spending levels. Why save money, only to find that it buys so much less than it would have even one year ago? Although inflation has cooled down since then, it periodically raises its avaricious head, and astute savers need to be alert to the threat.

COMBINED MOTIVES

For some savers, all of the savings motives fit together to make a complete financial plan. Looking ahead to retirement, it makes sense to save both for future security and future income. But even before retirement becomes foremost on the mind, savers will want to plan their savings with several motives in mind.

RUTH'S REASONS TO SAVE

Take the case of Ruth E., a single woman whose early life had been full of sadness. But by having faith in her own intelligence, by saving, and by following a conservative financial plan, Ruth changed the entire fabric of her life.

Ruth and her brothers and sisters had grown up on an isolated farm. Their father kept his family away from other people so that he could continue his abusive ways out of the sight of friends or neighbors. On many nights, Ruth's father sat at the kitchen table playing with a pistol, threatening that he would shoot any child who made a noise. He sometimes hung an effigy from a tree in the yard as a reminder of the power he held over the family and of what could happen if they didn't obey him completely.

It probably was no surprise to her mother and siblings when Ruth, the eldest, ran away from home at the first opportunity. She was 16 and felt she would now be able to work and claim her independence. She was hired as a waitress at a truck stop, where the manager allowed her to live on the premises. Not long after, she met a young Air Force sergeant and they were married.

To their disappointment, Ruth wasn't able to have children, so the couple, while serving in a foreign country, initiated adoption procedures for two young brothers from a local orphanage. But soon after, Ruth's husband was killed in an airplane crash. According to the laws of the country, a single woman could not complete adoption. She lost, along with everything else, the sons she had come to love.

Furthermore, the military widow's settlement was based largely on family status. She was given a modest insurance settlement, but since she had no children, she wasn't able to collect her husband's Social Security benefits until she reached retirement age.

With only a small amount of money, no education, no credit record in her own name, and no family, she had to begin her life over again.

Ruth started out very carefully, sharing an apartment with a friend and working at an entry-level position. She began to establish a credit record by buying a watch on lay-away at a small jewelry store. When she had proved that she was able to meet her payment schedule the store issued her a credit card. She made further small purchases and paid off whatever balance she had every month, thus avoiding interest payments but establishing a credit record. Soon she was able to buy a car, and at the same time she regularly added to her savings account.

By shopping for repossessed property, Ruth eventually was able to buy a duplex, easier since she could live in one half and rent out the other. This led to an unexpected break: One of her renters, a young single woman, became pregnant and decided to give up her child for adoption. Because she was now in the U.S., Ruth, as a single person, was able to legally adopt the baby.

Ruth continued to work and save, adding another and another property to her portfolio. Though by now she had worked her way up to a higher position, Ruth left her job to manage her own rentals full-time. She then was able to continue her education, and graduated from an adult school program at the head of her class.

At last report, Ruth was still saving money and working on her dreams. She hoped to find another child to adopt, and she was attending college part-time. She had made up her mind while still a teenager not to let outside events, whether they be poverty or personal tragedy, control her destiny. Being a smart and steady saver allowed her to stick to that decision.

Fortunately, not many of us have such serious burdens as she. But Ruth's success shows that people can lift themselves up from adversity, and that a savings plan can be the wings that offer flight.

CHANGING OLD HABITS

For most Americans, the problem is simpler, but a challenge nonetheless. We need to get control of spending habits, plot a savings plan, and make these changes part of a lifelong financial strategy. It may sound straightforward, but habits are tough to alter.

SAVING WILL BECOME CHIC

In an encouraging note, *Changing Times's* Theodore Miller pointed out, " . . . every economic excess breeds a corrective reaction, . . ." The reaction to the high level of consumption and excessive borrowing of the past will be a conservative adjustment—that of saving more.

America seemed to start getting that message near the end of the 1980s, according to Imperial Corporation's Charlotte Wingfield: "We are just beginning to move out of the credit cycle into the savings cycle. I see more and more baby boomers coming to Imperial than I did even three years ago. Three years ago all they wanted was another credit card. The stock market [crash of 1987] impacted that tremendously. All those youngsters who thought they could get rich quick know they need a safe vehicle for retirement money."

Additionally, many need to buy homes, educate children and live as comfortable lives as possible. Seizing control of borrowing and saving habits is an essential first step.

CHAPTER 2

The Price of Borrowing; The Promise of Saving

"Most people fail to concentrate on the difference between making money and keeping it."

ELIOT JANEWAY, *Prescription for Prosperity*

Shakespeare may have warned, neither a borrower nor a lender be, but William didn't live in the 20th century. Borrowing, when used judiciously, can help consumers live better daily lives. It can be a wonderful tool in long-term planning and wealth-building.

NOT ALL BORROWING IS BAD

When tax laws treat borrowing in a preferential way, as they do with home mortgage interest, there can be monetary advantages to carrying a safe level of debt. And in times of racing inflation, many consumers prefer to make purchases when prices are lower, then pay back their loans with less valuable dollars. But however wise for durable types of purchases, the idea of using credit to beat inflation can be nothing more than a justification for overspending when it comes to paying for a night on the town or a new necktie.

GIVE THE CARDS A LITTLE CREDIT

Even that national nemesis, the credit card, has some value to consumers. They are an excellent source of free credit and invaluable as a source of emergency cash.

SMART LOANS

And as for lending, it probably still is prudent to keep a curb on loans to a profligate business associate or to a video-game crazed, teen nephew. But lending can remarkably shrewd when the loan is made to:

- The government, in the guise of a Treasury Bill or some other security
- A financial institution, in the form of a certificate of deposit
- Someone buying real estate from you in the structure of a first mortgage or first trust deed (watch out for second mortgages, which may end up worthless in case of default)
- A high-quality corporation as a bond
- Any number of other safety-oriented financial instruments

THE CRUELTY OF CREDIT

Still, when abused, credit can be a Shylock that demands its pound of flesh. And borrowers who play too loose and free with plastic cash or loans of any kind may need someone as eloquent as Portia to speak on their behalves when they land in court.

While most borrowers don't go so far that they get into legal difficulties, few people realize what a drain interest rate charges can be on monthly budgets.

A COSTLY HABIT

Take credit card charges, for instance. The 25-day interest-free grace period is a privilege granted only to those who pay their monthly bills in full. If balances are carried over from month to month, interest on most credit card accounts starts accruing as soon as a purchase is made.

Furthermore, deductions of credit card interest for income tax purposes are disappearing. That deduction will be phased out by 1990, points out the American Institute of Certified Public Accountants. "Paying for the privilege of buying what you want now is a lot more expensive than you may realize," cautions the institute. "Credit card interest rates vary from 18 to 22 percent per year. If your bank charges 19 percent and your monthly unpaid balance over a year totals $6,000, interest payments add up to a whopping $1,140."

TIME TAKES ITS TOLL

For installment payments, money also grows more costly over time. For the borrower, the longer the term of the loan, the poorer the deal it is likely to be. You would pay $2,683.20 more in interest on a five-year, $10,000 loan at an interest levy of 12 percent than you would on a three-year loan for the same amount, according to *Money* magazine.

THE SIREN'S CALL

While interest rate charges represent a drain on financial resources, an even greater danger is spending more than was budgeted for consumer purchases—simply because it's so easy to do. According to Donald Badders, president of the National Foundation For Consumer Credit, burgeoning credit card balances have become a serious problem for some people. Just as there are those who can become addicted to cigarettes, drugs, or gambling, some can become compulsive

---

Table 2–1
The Cost of Interest at Various Rates and Terms

Full interest cost for $1,000 of credit if paid back in equal monthly installments.

Annual Percentage Rate (APR)	1Yr.	2 Yrs.	3 Yrs.	4 Yrs.	5 Yrs.
12%	$ 66.08	$129.68	$195.56	$236.84	$334.40
15%	83.00	163.52	247.76	335.84	426.80
18%	100.04	198.08	301.40	409.76	523.40
21%	117.32	233.12	356.12	486.08	623.00

---

credit card chargers. Badders told the Associated Press that while the number of "debt-dogged consumers" has remained pretty much the same, the size of their debt is "a lot deeper than it was 10 years ago."

The average person counseled at Badders's foundation in 1980 had about $9,000 in accumulated debt, compared with $15,000 in 1987 and $17,000 in 1988. Credit card debt, he added, is the largest growing component of consumer debt.

A HOUSE OF CARDS

A particularly ominous form of consumer borrowing, warns Jane Bryant Quinn, is one that taps into home equity to back a line of credit. "A home-equity line of credit is a second mortgage against your home," Quinn pointed out in her "Staying Ahead" column. "You might have $25,000 to $50,000 worth of borrowing power, for everything from home improvements to a weekend at Vail."

Some banks give customers a special checkbook for accessing home equity, but some also give credit cards. "Studies have shown that people use credit cards far more casually than cash," Quinn said. "If it's plastic, it doesn't seem like real money. Given a credit line of $50,000, and a plastic card, a spendaholic can do himself out of house and home—literally."

THE COST OF LOST OPPORTUNITY

In addition to the factors that make overuse of credit dangerous, the lost opportunity, while less ominous, must be considered. Those dollars spent on interest payments for non-essential purchases would add up to a substantial amount, if they had been saved or put to other uses.

THE MIRACULOUSLY EVAPORATING MORTGAGE

When alternatives to spending include reducing overall mortgage payments, the results can be startling. Steres Alpert & Carne, an accounting firm based in San Diego, calculates that $10,000, $25,000, $50,000, or more can be saved by paying off a home mortgage early.

"Strange as it may sound, you can save money by paying a little extra each month when you make your mortgage payment," the CPA firm points out. "The additional amount goes toward reducing the amount of principal remaining on the loan. The smaller the principal, the less interest you pay over the life of the loan. It's as simple as that."

The firm offers an example of the actual dollar savings from a series of payments: "For simplicity, say you take out a new $150,000 mortgage at a fixed interest rate of 10 percent, payable in 30 years (or 360 months). In round numbers, your monthly mortgage payment (principal and interest, not including property taxes) figures to be $1,316."

If you live in the home for 30 years, figures the accounting firm, you will be paying out nearly $474,000 to the lender—including approximately $324,500 in interest.

But something amazing happens if the mortgage holder pays an extra $100 per month, starting with the first monthly mortgage payment. In that case, the interest paid over the life of the loan comes to $215,758–$108,810 less than with the original terms of the home loan. In addition, the house will be paid off about 8½ years sooner than if the extra payments were not made.

"Keep this in mind: The more money you can afford to prepay, the greater your savings," explains Steres Alpert & Carne. "And the sooner you start, the more you will save. Reminder: you pay a higher percentage of interest in the early years of the mortgage."

However, when the interest deduction for mortgages allowed by the Internal Revenue Service is considered, the savings would be somewhat smaller. Assuming that the homebuyer in the example remains in a 28 percent tax bracket for the 30 years of the loan, the buyer would be able to save an extra $30,467 in taxes if the prepayment weren't made. Even so, the overall savings would come to $78,343— nothing to sneeze at for most homeowners.

MEASURE ALL ALTERNATIVES

The CPA firm does point out, however, that home loan prepayment does not make sense if the rate of return possible on an investment is higher than the interest rate of the loan. For example, if your mortgage interest is only 9 percent, but money market funds are paying 11 percent, it is wiser to put the extra $100 cited in the example in the money market fund, until investment rates fall below 9 percent.

And of course it makes no sense at all to pay off a mortgage early if consumer debt carrying a higher interest rate remains outstanding.

MINDING THE STORE

If avoiding interest payments when they aren't absolutely necessary is part of good financial planning, earning interest and managing those interest earnings can lead to spectacular gains.

Even a seemingly insignificant percentage point in rates can make a very big difference in earnings, especially if the account is held over long period of time, such as a college fund or an Individual Retirement Account may be.

Whether the yield on a certificate of deposit is 8.33 percent or 9.80 percent, for example, is significant. A $10,000 investment held for 30 years, at the lower rate, may be worth $110,271, and at the higher rate, $165,223. If $2,000 were deposited each of 30 years at the 8.33 percent rate, the fund could be worth $260,800; at 9.8 percent, it could be worth $347,826.

CONSEQUENCES OF COMPOUNDING

Yields at a given rate may differ because of the way the account is compounded. Compounding can occur daily, monthly, quarterly, semiannually, or annually.

If that $10,000 in the preceding example were earning 10 percent compounded daily, the account would grow to $75,962 in 20 years, bringing a true yield of 10.67 percent. If it were only compounded annually, however, the final

Table 2–2
How Earned Interest Compounds at Various Rates

If $10,000 were saved for 30 years and compounded annually, the result would be as follows at the end of each five-year period.

	5th Yr.	10th Yr.	15th Yr.	20th Yr.	25th Yr.	30th Yr.
6%	$13,382	$17,908	$23,965	$32,071	$ 42,918	$ 57,434
7%	14,025	19,671	27,590	38,696	54,274	76,122
8%	14,693	21,589	31,721	46,609	68,484	100,626
9%	15,386	23,673	36,424	56,044	86,230	132,676
10%	16,105	25,937	41,772	67,274	108,347	174,494
11%	16,850	28,394	47,845	80,623	135,854	228,922
12%	17,623	31,058	54,735	96,462	170,000	299,599

balance becomes $67,274 at the end of the 20 years (See Table 2.2.)

The more often earnings are paid to the saver (compounded to or added onto the principal) the faster the account grows. This is because compounding allows the interest earned to collect interest earnings of its own.

THAT TATTLER, TIME

The sooner one starts saving, the better off one will be. "Assuming a return of 9.02 percent (the average annual return for the stock market during the past 20 years) here's the effect time has on money," points out California financial planner W. Scott Wiley of Waddell & Reed Financial Services. "If a 25 year old wanted to have $1 million at age 65 for retirement, he would have to save about $212 per month for 40 years. However, if that individual waited until age 30, his savings must be $338 per month. That savings of $126 per month (60 percent less) is the benefit that an investor gains by using time as a tool during that five-year period to grow investments."

All this potential earnings from money that simply sits quietly and behaves itself!

SOUL-SEARCHING ABOUT SAVING

As the national debate rages over whether the U.S. savings rate is too high, too low, or just where it ought to be, American consumers need to be conducting a personal debate.

"Is my own savings rate what it ought to be?" should be the first question, but it should be followed by others. "What do I want and need my money to do for me this year? Five years from now? At retirement?" And finally, consumers should be asking, "How do I get where I need to be from where I am now?"

Very few people save as much as they should, and a fair number have no idea how to get from the precarious position of saving too little to the abundance that adequate saving can offer.

YOU CAN DO IT TOO

It is possible to transform tragic saving habits into magic habits, but too many people just don't know where to begin. Where will the money come from to make regular contributions to a savings account?

Keep in mind the words of Goethe: "Whatever you can do or dream you can do, begin it. Boldness has genius, power, and magic in it." Even if savers have to start small, it's important to start soon. Almost anyone can find some way to stash cash.

PART
2

How
to
Save

CHAPTER 3

Where to Find the Money: Budgeting

"For of all sad words of tongue or pen
The saddest are these: "It might have been."

MAUD MULLER WHITTIER

Sally L. was a single mother of two children. She worked in the delicatessen section of a supermarket. Her ex-husband hadn't paid child support in almost a decade, but each year, Sally was able to save something from her modest salary so that she and the children could have a vacation together.

How did she do it? She figured out how much the vacation would cost, and divided that amount by 52 to determine how much she would need to save in each weekly pay period. She the put the money aside each week in her credit union savings account, even if it meant taking a sack lunch to work or wearing socks to bed so she could turn off the electric blanket. To Sally, the two weeks of relaxation and fun with her son and daughter made budgeting for the remainder of the year well worth small sacrifices.

If Sally could do it, almost anyone else can.

BUT I OWE TOO MUCH!

But, you say, I'm already so deeply in debt that I'd be better off spending the vacation money on paying down some of those credit accounts. Right after her divorce, Sally had been in the same sort of fix. She realized that before she could move forward, she would have to stop moving backwards.

When a budget is in that catastrophic condition, it cries out for curative action, preferably before personal bankruptcy becomes the only option.

DANGER SIGNS

The thought of bankruptcy may be shocking, but more and more Americans face that reality each year. If the following signs are present, cautions the Consumer Credit Institute, bankruptcy court may be on the horizon:

- Not paying bills on time, or juggling bill-paying each month
- Making only minimum payments on large credit card bills
- Not knowing how much you owe
- Living up to two incomes, without putting anything aside for emergencies
- Regularly using your overdraft credit on your checking account to pay bills
- Being denied credit because of a negative credit report

The presence of one or more of the warning signs can spell trouble. The steps toward recovery require scrupulous self-honesty. A brutal examination of spending patterns is necessary. Do you go out and buy something to get yourself out of a blue mood? Does shopping with certain friends invariably lead to spending more money than intended? Have you created a public image that depends on showy clothes, extravagant restaurants, and an expensive car?

It sometimes seems that life would hold no pleasure, wouldn't be worth living, unless we can continue with some of the habits that get us in trouble. But alternatives can be found to almost every bad habit. Surely there are other mood-lifters, such as a walk in the country or inviting a dear friend in for tea, that can be called upon. Perhaps you and your friend can schedule a shopping trip to a swap meet rather than to Saks Fifth Avenue. And believe it or not, you'll find just as many friends and fascinating things to do when you're conserving money. In fact, the less-costly choices can add the spice to life.

SALVATION

Like any journey, the trek to financial solidarity, whether it begins from a balanced budget or one that is deep in red ink, is made one milestone at a time:

- First comes the decision to take action.
- Then begins the collection of information and knowledge.
- Next, goals are set.
- Finally, hazy dreams begin to take shape. Some dreams actually come true, and it now becomes clear that the achievement of goals is possible.

STARTING OUT

If the decision has been made to save more money, but the first step is to escape from overwhelming debt, here is where to start:

- Analyze where your money is going by keeping records, then establish a budget and stick to it.
- Contact your creditors if you are facing temporary problems in making your payments. Try to work out a repayment schedule that you can meet. (This is what

foreign countries and corporations do when you hear that they have "restructured" their debt.)

- If the problem is severe or long-term, contact a credit counseling service. To find a reputable one, call the Better Business Bureau.
- If you're considering whether to file for bankruptcy, first seek competent legal advice. Because of its legal and financial consequences, bankruptcy should be considered only in extreme situations. Be aware that there are fees associated with filing, and you must, contrary to popular belief, pay some or all of your debts.

THAT PESKY PLASTIC

If the trouble stems from credit cards, that easy-spending plastic cash, just about the only way to reduce debt is to cut back on spending. It may help to put away those cards that aren't absolutely necessary. You may want to keep a card issued by your favorite department store, but stick it in a desk drawer at home and take it out only when you've made a rational decision to buy something.

THE CREDIT CARETAKER

While credit cards may be troublesome to some people, anyone who has tried to rent a car without a major credit card or to finance a home without a credit record, knows that it is essential to have at least one card in current working order. That's the nature of today's society.

The American Financial Services Association offers these rules of thumb for managing credit:

- Borrow only for items that will make a significant contribution to your family and its life style. The word to emphasize in that sentence is *significant*.
- Borrow only if you are currently spending significantly less each month than you make and if that cushion

can carry the proposed debt without curtailing regular savings and other necessities.

DEBT LIMITS

Many experts say no more than 15 percent to 20 percent of monthly net income should be allocated to repayment of installment loans, not including mortgage payments. And remember, this is the upper limit. It may be prudent to stick to 10 percent or less.

Even while working your way out of debt, set aside some savings. Even as small a reserve as 3 percent to 5 percent monthly can help establish the saving habit.

STARTING A BUDGET

A clear picture of your financial status requires four basic steps:

Step 1. List all income.
Step 2. Track all current expenses.
Step 3. From that information, develop a budget as a master plan for future spending.
Step 4. Check your progress periodically.

INVENTORY OF INCOME

Probably the easiest of these four steps is the listing of income. Salaries and wages come first.

The budget worksheet on page 26 (Figure 3-1) can serve as a guide. Use take-home pay only, when listing salaries and commissions, since this worksheet makes no provisions for income tax, or the withholding of Social Security, disability insurance, or any of the other government-required deductions from paychecks.

Those who receive commissions or gratuities should list the average income from these sources; if in doubt, err on

Figure 3-1   **Budget Worksheet**

Budget Worksheet

NOTE: Record both monthly and annual expenses. Divide the annual by 12 to get the amount you should be setting aside each month, and multiply monthly expenses by 12 to get the total you will spend for the year.
   This chart was created to apply to as many financial situations as possible. Some categories may not apply to you. Ignore these and focus on those which reflect your financial status.

Item	Av. Mo Expense	Total Year Expense		Av. Mo. Expense	Total Year Expense		Av. Mo Expense	Total Year Expense
SHELTER			HEALTH CARE			SAVINGS		
Rent or mortgage payment			Physicians, dentists			Savings Accounts		
Property taxes			Drugs (inc. non-prescription)			Life insurance		
Property insurance			Health/hospital insurance			Disability insurance		
Maintenance			Hospital costs			Investments		
Gas. oil. electricity			Other			Retirement contributions		
Telephone			PERSONAL CARE			Other		
Water and sewer			Hair care			OBLIGATIONS		
Other			Toiletries			Alimony/Child support		
FOOD			Personal care appliances			Child care		
Groceries			Pocket money allowances			Credit card payments		
Meals away from home			Other			Other debt payments		
Tobacco Products/Alcohol			RECREATION			EDUCATION		
Other			Vacations			Education/training expenses		
TRANSPORTATION			Recreational equipment			TOTAL EXPENDITURES		
Car payments			Recreational activities					
Gasoline. oil. etc			Movies. theatre			INCOME		
Maintenance. repair			Parties hosted in home			All salaries and wages		
Auto insurance			Newspapers. books. etc			Average commission income		
Public transportation			Club dues			Average part-time work		
Carpool costs			Other			Alimony/Child support		
Taxes and fees			GIFTS & CONTRIBUTIONS			Dividends/interest		
Other			Religious and charities			Pension/Social Security		
CLOTHING			Political causes			Other		
New purchases			Family gifts			TOTAL INCOME		
Dry cleaning/laundry			Non-family gifts					
Mending. repair			Christmas gifts			TOTAL EXPENDITURES		
Other			Other			BALANCE		

By Frances B. Smith

Consumer Finance Bulletin is published monthly as a public service by the Consumer Credit Institute of the American Financial Services Association, 1101 14th St., N.W., Washington, D.C. 20005. AFSA represents firms that provide financial services to consumers and small businesses. Please call Frances B. Smith (202) 289-0400, Director, Consumer Credit Institute, for further information.

Reprinted by permission of the Consumer Credit Institute, the consumer education arm of the American Financial Services Association, Washington, D.C.

the conservative side. Nothing demolishes a financial plan faster than overestimating resources.

INADEQUATE INCOME

If at the end of the budgeting exercise you realize that your income simply isn't enough to cover your fixed expenses, consider finding either a better-paying job or supplemental part-time employment.

Don't feel like a failure if you simply don't earn enough money. Only about 37 percent of U.S. households have the income required to qualify for a loan to buy an average-priced house, according to Kenneth Leventhal & Co., a real estate company.

When insufficient income is a chronic problem, think about changing careers, even if it requires returning to school to train for a higher-paying job. Throughout history, the highest return of any investment has been realized from money spent for education.

Even so, your long-term earnings prospects may be more distinguished than you realize. Table 3-1 demonstrates how much you will earn over a long period of time if your income remains constant. The trick, of course, is keeping some of that for yourself.

Table 3-1
Earnings Outlook

Monthly Income	10 Yrs.	20 Yrs.	30 Yrs.	40 Yrs.
$1,000	$120,000	$240,000	$ 360,000	$ 480,000
1,500	180,000	360,000	540,000	720,000
2,000	240,000	480,000	720,000	960,000
2,500	300,000	600,000	900,000	1,200,000
3,000	360,000	720,000	1,080,000	1,440,000
3,500	420,000	840,000	1,260,000	1,680,000
4,000	480,000	960,000	1,440,000	1,920,000

TRACKING EXPENSES

True, it's a pain in the neck to keep detailed records of spending. But you'll be glad you do it.

A New York couple with an income of $100,000 per year were puzzled that they weren't able to save money, until they chronicled their cash outflow. They discovered they were paying $26,000 a year on restaurant meals.

Filling in some of the blanks on the budget worksheet is easy. For rent, utilities, telephone costs, car payments, and child support payments the exact amount is either clearly registered in most people's minds or their checkbooks, or easy to look up. Other expenses, such as car repairs, charitable contributions and education expenses, require some detective work. Generally these payments are made by check, credit card, or payroll deductions; dig around in the paperwork and they will come forward.

But most people don't know how much, exactly, they spend on lunches, gifts, entertainment, clothes, toiletries and the like. Here's where the hard part comes.

DEAR DIARY

Keep a log of daily spending—at least long enough to see spending patterns take shape. Maintain an expense journal for a month at the minimum, since many expenditures, such as haircuts are made only occasionally. "Penny wise and pound foolish" may seem like an outdated concept, but it's amazing how much money can be frittered away on small items.

If you begin recording expenses in November or December, continue the recordkeeping on through January and February to obtain a clearer picture of spending patterns. The last two months of the year, which usually are laden with holiday shopping, are hardly representative of the remaining ten months.

One budgeter discovered, for example, that she was paying a ridiculous amount for parking tickets. Always in a hurry and a little lax about keeping track of time, Donna G. often found little greetings from the city on her windshield. She always paid them fast so that the fines didn't multiply. It didn't seem like a lot of money. But after tracking expenditures, Donna realized that she was averaging a ticket per month. At $15 each, that came to $180 a year. And Donna had been wondering where she would find the money for a new winter coat.

THE CHECKBOOK TRICK

A trick to making accountability less of a chore is to pay for anything over $10 by check. If the expense will be tax-deductible, put a small star in your check record when you list the item.

Once the habit of recordkeeping is begun, it's not so hard to maintain. And the revelations, the enlightenment, the exposure to self-knowledge will be well worth the effort.

BUILDING A BUDGET

Again, the budget worksheet can be useful in constructing a financial plan. At first, it helped by delineating how much money was being spent and where it was going.

Start now with a clean slate. In its next function, the worksheet can be used to create the ideal world—to identify how much *should* be spent, and where the spending *should* be allocated.

TEAM TACTICS

Setting goals and creating a budget is difficult for individuals, and it may be even more problematic for dual-income couples. But planning for working couples is even more important, lest the second income become a tax liability rather than an income advantage.

"Communication is vital," says the American Financial Services Association. "Even if the combined income is high, both husband and wife should jointly form, and adhere to, a spending plan that should include discussions about making major purchases."

The AFSA offers these tips for two-paycheck families:

- It's always wise to regard both salaries as income to the family. It's an ill-advised spouse who regards his or her income as "personal money."
- Borrowing to finance a major purchase—a car or appliance—should be a joint decision, regardless of who the user will be. Avoid debt levels that will demand the full earning potential of both wage earners.
- Personal allowances for each spouse are essential. Everybody should have money to spend as he or she chooses. Agree on an amount and make the money available routinely.
- Be sure to include an agreed-upon savings plan.

While each individual or family will work out budgets that fit unique standards and style, it is helpful to have some yardsticks against which to measure individual budgets.

DIVIDING UP THE MONEY—
A FISCAL FRAMEWORK

It is difficult to say how much someone should spend on housing, food, or medical or utility costs, since these expenditures depend on the size and general health of the family, geographic location, and factors in the economy over which the individual may have little or no control. However, most experts recommend that no more than 65 percent of take-home pay should be designated for fixed monthly expenses, including food, car payments, utilities, and rent or house payments. Allow another 20 percent for such variable

31

expenses as household and automobile repairs, recreation, and clothing. Put aside 10 percent for necessary expenses that hit at regular intervals, such as car insurance and income taxes. At the very minimum, 5 percent should be earmarked for long-term saving; 10 percent would be better.

Another potential budget-buster is the automobile loan. If a car loan is more than 15 percent of your annual net income, (income after taxes and other mandatory payments are withheld) you're probably driving a vehicle that is above your means. Consider trading for a less-expensive car or buying a good-quality used automobile.

BEGIN WITH THE BIGGEST

Because the fixed monthly expenditures are the largest items in most budgets, decisions on how they should be handled should be made especially carefully. Changing apartments or houses frequently is not the easiest way to cut down on expenses. Moving costs could eat up most of the saving, on top of the loss of time and convenience. However, it may be the only way for some people to make financial progress.

When choosing a place to live, think of all the financial ramifications. The rent or mortgage of a suburban home may be less the farther the site is from work, but it's senseless to save $100 per month on housing only to then spend $200 per month more on transportation. Upkeep, utility costs (an electric versus a gas water heater?), and convenience to services should be taken into consideration when selecting a home.

MORTGAGE MANAGEMENT

When gauging ability to meet mortgage payments, most lenders figure that the average family can afford monthly payments for housing—including insurance, taxes, and utilities—of one-quarter to one-third of take home pay. For example, with net pay of $3,000 per month, housing costs should run from $833 to $1,000 monthly.

Another rule of thumb is that a buyer can afford a home priced at no more than 2½ times his or her annual gross salary. So with an annual income of $40,000, a person should be able to afford a house costing $100,000.

Almost nothing is more demoralizing to a family than to be strapped with house payments that are too big. The home, a place that should be enjoyed as a haven from the difficulties of the world, becomes an object of loathing. Couples feel trapped in the very place that was supposed to make them feel happy and secure.

From a psychological point of view, it's better to be in less of a house you can afford than more. Of course, the larger the down payment, the lower the house payments.

SAVING FOR A DOWN PAYMENT

A down payment of 20 to 30 percent of the purchase price is usually required, meaning the $40,000 wage earner would need to put aside $20,000 to $30,000 for initial equity.

When saving for that first down payment, it helps to be paying as little for rent as possible. A single person may take a roommate. A couple may find an apartment where they can pay lower rent in return for acting as on-site managers. Clever shoppers have been able to cut costs on everything from transportation to food to footwear. But more about cost-cutting later.

GUARDING AGAINST CALAMITY

Health, auto, and homeowners insurance should be reviewed carefully to make certain that coverage is sufficient and that rates compare favorably with other similar policies.

When allotting money for insurance, don't overlook the most crucial form of catastrophe protection for people in the wage-earning years—disability insurance. This often-slighted coverage pays monthly income if you are unable to work because of illness or injury. Disability insurance usually is available from lenders to cover consumer loan or mortgage payments should the borrower become disabled.

Statistics show that a person is much likelier at any given time to become disabled than to die, yet people pay more attention to life insurance than disability plans. "At age 42, for example, you are about four times more likely to be disabled for at least three months before retirement than you are to die," reports *Money* magazine. "In fact disability is sometimes called 'living death,' since your family's financial needs continue but you can't meet them unless you have income."

SAVING AT LAST?

There is always the temptation to leave saving for the last item in the budget—to put anything left over into the saving and investment category. That kind of planning leads to a budget with one or more of these pitfalls:

- The family can't live with it.
- Consumer debt gets out of hand.
- When finances are reviewed, it appears the family just never seems to get ahead.

SAVING IN SECTORS

While at first it may seem cumbersome to divide reserve funds into several different accounts, segregation may be the only way to keep funds from mingling to the point that you forget the purpose for which you intended them. It's also a sound way to keep your hands off of your long-term savings.

NEAR TERM

The first savings account might be designated for very short-term needs, such as birthday and holiday gifts, entertainment, and babysitting fees. Grandmother used to call it the cookie jar account, and that isn't a bad name for it. A simple savings account at a convenient bank, thrift, or credit union is a good place to stash the dough.

THE MIDDLE TERM

The second account is earmarked for savings with an intermediate life span. It is here that money accumulates for anticipated future needs such as domestic emergencies, down payments on cars and perhaps a home. The vacation fund as well goes in this account. A money market mutual fund that allows the writing of a few checks each month may be ideal for this account. If the fund for some reason grows quite large (you're nearly ready to make that down payment on the house), some of the money may be transferred to short-term certificates of deposit. That choice depends on how money market rates and CD rates compare.

THE LONGER TERM

Into a long-term account go "financial cushion" fund and retirement savings. These certainly should go into accounts of their own, since it is through these types of funds that a saver can best take advantage of higher interest rates for extended maturities. If possible, retirement money should be in a tax-deferred or tax-sheltered account. Because long-range money is so important to an individual's security, insured or very safe investment vehicles are preferred. (Retirement saving will be covered in additional detail in Chapter 6.)

This extended-term account is the core of your savings. The balances in the near-term and mid-term accounts fluctuate with time and circumstances. The long-term account does not vacillate in both directions—it only gets larger until true financial security has been achieved.

This nest egg is not to be spent until financial independence has arrived. "Use your accumulated assets for collateral for building a larger egg then a larger one," suggests author and financial planner Venita Van Caspel.

THE BOTTOM LINE

As a final step in budgeting, when total expenditures are subtracted from total income, the balance should be zero, or slightly on the positive side. If there is an excess, it may be possible to save more money or to reward yourself by allocating more funds to a chosen category.

If the sum is negative, it's time to go to work. If the deficit is small, judicious trimming here and there may be all that is necessary. In the upcoming section on savings plans, suggestions on where to find additional "hidden" money in the budget will be given.

FROM THEORY TO PRACTICE

Transforming a budget plan into action, one financial counselor noted, becomes easier if each action is related to an objective. "For example, singles and young couples may be looking for their first home, while those with children may be saving for the kids' education. Others may be at their peak earning period and able to accumulate relatively large sums presently. Still others may be planning for retirement income to supplement Social Security and pension benefits."

And, of course, goals change. Some objectives are achieved and need to be replaced with newer aims. Sometimes a goal will lose its relevance and should be updated. A couple may have been saving for a racy new sports car; but, surprise—they discover a baby is on the way. A small van may not seem as exciting as a Corvette, but it sure costs less, and it will accommodate a car seat.

A reevaluation of goals and of the strategy to meet those goals should be conducted regularly. The review and over-haul may best take place when checking to see how the budget is working.

MEASURING HEADWAY

Again, to know how you're doing, you have to know what you've done. Recordkeeping is essential. A real nuisance? Not when you realize that by your keeping monthly records, much of your work is already done when it's time to prepare for tax returns in January and February.

CLOSE MONITORING IN THE BEGINNING

In the first few months of living with a new budget, a review should take place monthly. Adjustments can be made to fine-tune the system. At the end of the first year, if all is going well, the status check should be made quarterly. At the end of the second year, the reassessment can be done annually, perhaps when tax returns have been completed.

You may need to incorporate changes in response to the ever-evolving income tax regulations. And be ready to review the budget anytime a change occurs that unavoidably impacts cash flow. A big promotion; the birth of another child; an out-of-town transfer; someone in the household either leaving work or getting a job—these and other big events call for a new look at the game plan.

TIPS FOR CONTROLLING THE SPENDING URGE

- If you tend to spend flamboyantly to lift yourself out of a bad mood, substitute something small but inspi-rational for a costlier item. Buy yourself a car-polisher rather than hiring a monthly detailing service, or sub-stitute a morning run in the park for a membership at a gymnasium. A bouquet of fresh flowers, a paperback book, or a cup of aromatic gourmet coffee at an outdoor cafe may chase the blues as effectively as a $300 food processor.

- If your friends have invited you to join them for lunch at an expensive restaurant, don't pass up the pleasure of their company. Instead, simply order an appetizer or a hearty bowl of soup, or arrange to split an order with a dieting friend. Often you can fill up on the bread that accompanies the meal. If you're still hungry, have a less expensive snack later in the day.

- Make it a hobby to know all the thrift stores, second-hand shops, and resale boutiques. It's silly to pay full price for Agatha Christie novels or the classics when they can be purchased for one-fourth the amount at a used book store. And it's not as if Christie or Dickens were coming out with a new novel that can only be bought new, in hard cover.

- Stick to the classics in clothes, furnishings, dishes, or anything else that can be trendy. You can use classic colors, patterns, and shapes much longer, and they tend to mix and match with more styles and shades. Achieve a contemporary look with haircuts, costume jewelry, place mats, or anything else that needs to be redone or replaced regularly.

- Take up a hobby that doubles as gift-giving. Learn to knit, do wood work, mold pottery, create jewelry or paint. It's not as silly as it may sound.

    Ben, who spends time each year clearing his property of fallen trees and underbrush, knows exactly what to do with the debris. He gives cords of wood and bundles of kindling for presents at Christmas, for birthdays, or on other special occasions. We all love a crackling fire in the fireplace.

- When going out as a couple, let the more frugal of the two carry the cash. Agree in advance how much you intend to spend, and make menu selections or whimsical purchases accordingly. If going out to dinner or a party where drinking will take place, the designated, non-drinking driver should be the money handler.

Finances in Serious Trouble?

If help is needed to salvage a budget or to avoid bankruptcy, these organizations may help:

The American Financial Services Association, 1101 Fourteenth St., NW, Washington, DC 20005. (202) 289-9400. For a small charge, AFSA will send The Consumer's Almanac, a useful calendar designed to keep a budget record.
Consumer Credit Institute, 1101 Fourteenth St., NW, Washington, DC 20005. (202) 289-9400.
National Foundation for Consumer Credit, Suite 507, 8701 Georgia St., Silver Spring, MD 20901

CHAPTER 4

How Much Should You Save?

"Some people regard discipline as a chore. For me, it is a kind of order that sets me free to fly."

JULIE ANDREWS

Sorry to do this, but the time has come again to evoke guilt feelings by comparing Americans with the Japanese. If good common sense and sound financial planning guidance have not spurred you to save, a dose of nationalism may do the job.

Here it is. Japan was the world's leader in per capita saving in 1988, beating out the Swiss for the second consecutive year, according to a survey by the International Savings Banks Institute.

AMAZING SAVINGS

Each Japanese citizen, on an average, had saved a total of $38,439 by the end of 1987, an increase of $11,136 from the previous year. For the same period, Switzerland, the long-time thriftiest nation, recorded per capita savings of $34,763, an increase of about $9,500.

Sure, you may say, but residents of these countries had the strong value of the yen and the Swiss franc on their side. And besides, you may persist, these are very small countries in which people live in tiny houses. They can't spend a lot of money, because they wouldn't have any place to store stuff if they bought it.

And there is consolation in knowing that the U.S. ranked above some countries. The Senegalese saved an average of $69 a year per person; Ethiopians only $18 and Nigerians a meager $7.

BUT MORE OF US BUY HOUSES

Enough of this remorse. The truth is, few citizens of the countries with impressively high savings rates have the percentage of home ownership that the U.S. does. And, unfortunately, though many people in this country use home ownership as a way to shelter income from taxes, to increase net worth, and to save for retirement needs, this reality is not reflected in the way the savings rate is calculated.

Our tendency to use a home for a savings vehicle is both admirable and unsatisfactory. It has advantages and disadvantages that will be discussed in the next chapter.

THIS ISN'T WHAT WAS MEANT BY "A CASHLESS SOCIETY"

It clearly is not enough to pour all spare money into a house or any single tangible asset. Being house-poor usually means a family has no cash reserves or financial cushion to:

- Protect an investment in that home
- Guard against unexpected events whether they be happy or tragic
- Help position members to take best advantage of opportunities as they come along

41

Cash accounts or cash-equivalent reserves are an essential part of a saving plan.

OK, SO HOW MUCH?

How much to save is an entirely personal decision. Some people are natural risk-takers; they are at ease with limited reserves and must be pushed or frightened into salting away more for the future. Others tend to lean in the opposite direction. Either experience or lessons taught by their parents have made them fearful of debt, and they must keep enormous amounts in the bank to feel secure.

THE SUPER SAVERS

Saving at astounding levels isn't always a sign of emotional insecurity, however.

Mel and Marsha were taken aside by his father for a good "talking to" the month before they were to be married. Dad was a child of the Great Depression and had a strong distrust of banks and borrowing. Still, he and his wife had been able to build a nice life for their family and comfortable retirement for themselves, without borrowing a cent.

He shared his secret with the young New Mexico couple, and though they had no inherent loathing of debt, they decided to follow in his footsteps. After all, it had worked out exceedingly well for mother and father.

"Start out small, then progress by steps," the father explained. The youngsters already had cars, but they were used and would need replacing eventually. So, dad explained, "Start making car payments to yourself right away. Put the money in a special account, get the best rate you can, and don't stop until you have what you need to buy a car."

Do the same with anything you need to buy, he counseled. Be a thrifty shopper and pay cash for everything. Fortunately, Mel and Marsha enjoyed savvy shopping and were handy with tools and equipment. They could do many car, clothing, and house repairs, so their living expenses could be modest if need be. And with his job as a sheriff's deputy and hers as a teacher's aide, they eventually did very well.

Their first try to buy a new car didn't work out as planned. The old one needed replacing before they had accumulated enough for a current model. Instead they purchased a late-model used car. But next time around they made it.

At the same time, they were working on buying their first home. Before the children started arriving, they both worked small second jobs, all the paychecks of which went into the house fund.

Their first purchase was a small but comfortable mobile home. They found a bargain, of course. Next they started saving for land, and eventually, they were able to build a starter house on their lot. In time, they added rooms, improved the landscaping, and created a lovely home, which they owned free and clear.

This was accomplished by the time they were 40. Mel eventually became the sheriff. Marsha went back to college and later became a school principal. The first half of their lives was spent working hard and watching nickels and dimes turn into dollars and dollars into ever larger denominations. The second half of their lives was taken up with enjoying exceptional financial freedom.

NOT A PLAN FOR MOST

Not everyone could or would want to do what Mel and Marsha did. In fact, even they probably would have fared better, overall, if they had used a home mortgage to shelter much of their income from taxes. But it was a personal choice, and they have enjoyed their lives.

Their example illustrates the kind of financial comfort that can be achieved by taking saving seriously. Most people aspire for less ambitious, but wholly achievable, savings goals.

43

PERCENTAGE WISE

Financial planners ordinarily advise budgeters to set aside a certain percentage of gross income for savings, based on age. According to broad guidelines proposed by some experts, a 25-year-old single person should save 15 percent to 20 percent of pre-tax income. A 40-year-old couple with children should try to save 10 to 15 percent of their salaries. Once most major purchases have been made, the children are raised, and retirement has arrived, a savings rate of about 7 percent is sufficient.

While these suggestions are helpful, there is no one-size-fits-all savings plan. Many people stray from the stereotypical patterns of life, doing things sooner than usual or later than was expected of them.

OUT OF STEP BUT ON THE TRACK

Some people start their families in their late teens or early twenties. Their children can be completely through college by the time the parents reach 45.

While Americans traditionally built families between the ages of 25 and 35, it is not uncommon today for couples to postpone child-bearing until their middle or late thirties or even into their forties. These couples may be well-heeled compared with the younger parents. They probably have owned a home long enough to build up equity and own other assets as well. But they don't have the gap between child-rearing and retirement during which to stick away some cash for the golden years.

And even those fabled golden years can be atypical. Lucky are they who can happily sail into retirement with their family responsibilities completely behind them. Some retirees are still taking care of their own elderly parents. And what about families with a handicapped child? Provisions for that child's security after the parents are gone will be important to the parents' peace of mind. Also, many older people share the responsibility of raising grandchildren. They may want to ensure that those youngsters can get an education as well.

A FLAWLESS FIT

What most people need is a tailor-made savings plan, one that meets specific objectives. How can a savings plan be custom-made to meet the unique needs of each budget-maker? This chapter and the next two will help explain how it's done.

TAKING CARE OF BASICS

Consider again the concept introduced in the previous chapter that no more than 65 percent of take-home pay should be devoted to fundamental living expenses such as housing, utilities, food, and transportation. Understand that this percentage is only a starting place. It represents maximum spending for these categories. If living expenses are less, that means it may be possible to establish a financial cushion and to reach savings objectives earlier.

POCKET CHANGE

Another 5 percent of income should be allocated to "spending money" for immediate, miscellaneous needs. These are non-fundamentals—haircuts, newspaper subscriptions, children's allowances, pet care, movies, and so forth. They vary in cost, they may be dispensable; but they are encountered frequently enough that the funds to pay for them can be kept in a checking account. There is no point in saving money that is around for such a short time.

THE THRIFTY TRIO

Three suggested savings accounts were outlined in the budgeting process:

- Short-term
- Middle-term
- Long-term

It's important to remember that, while minimum contributions to each will be recommended, these accounts are flexible and expandable. They stretch and bend with individual life patterns.

BRIEFLY BUDGETED

For the typical individual or family, about 10 percent of all expenses needs to be earmarked for short-term savings, a relatively small, easy-to-reach account.

The guidelines for managing this account include a great deal of flexibility.

- Items for which withdrawals will be made are specific— Christmas shopping, for example, starts in October, so that is the time to transfer some funds.
- Money is taken from this account fairly frequently. It's OK; the money is there to help buy school clothes, pay the taxes and car insurance, and enjoy a night out on the town.

A younger man who dates frequently and has an active social life, for instance, may want to keep more than 15 percent of his net salary in this account. And that is acceptable as long as at least the minimum amounts are deposited into accounts number two and three.

MIDDLE MANAGEMENT

When we consider the mid-range savings account and the long-term account, the calculations become more complex and, at the same time, more personalized.

46

Figure 4-1   Future Goals Control Sheet

Future Goals Control Sheet
(A Family Spending Spread Sheet)

Put the total you will need on the "Goal" line under the month it will be needed. Then on the "Plan" line show how much must be set aside each month to have that total by that month.

SHORT RANGE GOALS (Under 12 months)		Jan	Feb	Mar	Apr	May	June	July	Aug	Sept	Oct	Nov	Dec
1. Taxes	Goal												
	Plan												
2. Vacation	Goal												
	Plan												
3. Home recreation equip.	Goal												
	Plan												
4. Furniture	Goal												
	Plan												
5. Minor appliances	Goal												
	Plan												
6. Home insurance	Goal												
	Plan												
7. Auto insurance	Goal												
	Plan												
8. Personal insurance	Goal												
	Plan												
9. Other insurance	Goal												
	Plan												
10. Christmas expense	Goal												
	Plan												
11.	Goal												
	Plan												
12.	Goal												
	Plan												

MIDDLE RANGE GOALS (1 through 5 years)	Mo. Av.	Total Each Year 19_	19_	19_	19_	19_	19_	19_	19_	19_	19_	19_	19_
13. Home improvement													
14. Boat or other rec. equip.													
15. HIS additional education													
16. HER additional education													
17. Automobile purchase													
18. Special trip													
19. Major appliances													
20.													
21.													
22.													

LONG RANGE GOALS (Over 5 years)	Mo. Av.	Total Each Year 19_	19_	19_	19_	19_	19_	19_	19_	19_	19_	19_	19_
23. College for #1													
24. College for #2													
25. College for #3													
26. Other college													
27. Purchase home													
28. Weddings													
29. Retirement													
30. Vacation home													
31. Other													
32.													

Until age 40, plan to put 15 percent of the budget into the intermediate account, and 5 percent into the long-term account.

- Remember, the intermediate account is to help buy a house, buy cars, purchase appliances, do remodeling jobs, and other such higher-ticket expenditures.
- Vacation money goes here too. But the amount of money to be spent on the holiday needs to be specified and controlled. To be as relaxing and refreshing as a vacation should be, it helps if the vacationer knows that the good time isn't destroying the financial master plan.
- No nipping into this fund to buy new clothes or a special gift! As the size of the account grows and the term it is held increases, stronger self-discipline is required.

The money for mid-range expenses must be fairly accessible, but it need not be in a so-called transaction account, in which any amount of money is available at any time. Certificates of deposit with varying and staggered maturities can be utilized by people who want their funds in government-insured accounts. A money market mutual fund is another place to keep these funds, though mutual funds are not federally insured. In future chapters, the risks, rewards and characteristics of each type of account will be explained.

Between age 40 and 45, the percentage of funds designated for the intermediate account should be decreased by one percentage point per year, while the portion allocated to the long-term account should be increased by one percentage point.

LIFE SAVINGS

From age 45 to 65, at least 10 percent of gross income should go to the long-term savings account—the one designated for a financial cushion and for retirement. This is true even for a person who opts for early retirement. With ever-increasing life expectancies, people should plan to provide for themselves well into their seventies and even beyond.

Also to be treated as long-term savings is money earmarked for higher education for children. However, there are special ways to save for your children's college, and those will be covered in subsequent chapters.

After age 65, if a retiree is financially secure, provisions for the long-term savings account can fall back to 5 percent. At this phase of life, the financial cushion should be maintained. Cautionary money to cover lengthy or catastrophic illness or disability should be kept on hand in the intermediate-term account. But at last, it's time to think of using and enjoying those retirement funds.

MIND THOSE MINIMUMS

As explained earlier, the table offered here is a model, to be used as a practical pattern for building wealth. The percentages should be seen as minimums. If an individual or family is able to allocate a larger percentage of income to savings, the extra amount should be assigned to the appropriate endowment.

Single people who are earning handsomely, but planning to be married later, may want to save as much in their long-term accounts (financial cushion and retirement funds) as possible while they are able. When children arrive, it then

Table 4-1
Lifetime Savings Schedule

Category of Savings	Up to Age 40	Age 40 to 45	Age 45 to 65	Age 65+
Short-term	10%	10%	10%	10%
Intermediate-term	15%	Down 1%/year	10%	15%
Long-term	5%	Up 1%/year	10%	5%

may be necessary to trim retirement savings to minimum levels.

The progression to a higher percentage of extended-term savings can be made earlier if it seems comfortable to do so. An unmarried person or childless couple in their peak earning years may find it entirely possible. The extra capital may provide the option of early retirement, a mid-life career change, launching into business on one's own, or any number of other personal choices.

PAY YOURSELF FIRST

Whatever the life phase or age group, saving should become a priority, a basic part of any budget. And it should never be forgotten—the earlier savings is started, the more that can be accomplished and the sooner financial security will be reached.

MAINTAINING A FINANCIAL CUSHION

Salespeople have long been counseled by their peers that in order to survive the whims of economic cycles or to last out a persistent stretch of bad luck, a reserve fund sufficient to cover financial needs for three to six months should be stockpiled and put into a safe haven.

This is a healthy target for everyone. It isn't something that is easily achieved by a person with an average income, but it is possible. The cushion can be considered a landmark amount, and when it is reached there is cause to celebrate. It means that a laudatory level of financial independence has been attained.

MANAGING A WINDFALL

The first step in managing an inheritance, lottery win, insurance settlement, or any other lump-sum windfall is reserving a financial cushion. Set aside what is needed for three to six months of living expenses in a secure, relatively liquid account. The interest earnings on that account should keep the amount current, as inflation constantly escalates the cost of living.

It is a good idea to keep the financial cushion intact, even when collecting what seems to be an adequate sum in retirement pensions. Perhaps the greatest worry of older people is the possibility that a prolonged and costly illness will deplete savings and then begin to erode current income. The cushion offers some financial protection, in the event that this should happen.

After the cushion is resolutely in place, reserves can be placed in increasingly diversified financial instruments, ones that enhance the balance and growth of a portfolio. None of the funds, however, should be tied up for more than three to five years.

FOUR CORNERS

The question of how to invest the various savings accounts will be addressed in more detail in future chapters. For now it is sufficient to say that the four major objectives for investing the funds are those of the classic investment portfolio:

- Safety
- An appropriate level of liquidity
- Income
- Growth

BROADENING THE HORIZONS

With the three levels of savings firmly in place and peace of mind provided by the cushion, successful savers have reached the point where they can start enjoying more elaborate vacations, perhaps aim for a luxury car, or treat themselves to something they've been longing to have.

After achieving these basic savings aims, it may be wise to continue saving, but to do so with the surplus going into an account that has been invested so as to boost current income or plump up retirement income.

THE GOLDEN EGG

Saving, by its very nature, implies accumulating money for a specific purpose, for buying something, as reserves against troubled times or as a retirement nest egg. But when savings goals have been achieved, when a sufficient amount of security has been attained, it is then appropriate to turn to investing, estate-building and serious charitable giving.

Just as it is a wise individual who knows when and how to save, it is a well-balanced person who knows when and how to use and enjoy the wealth that has been created.

CHAPTER 5

Best Ways to Save

"Can anybody remember when the times were not hard and money not scarce?"

RALPH WALDO EMERSON

Once the decision has been made to be a better saver, a way must be found to retrieve that money from the hungry jaws of a checking account. When mingled with other funds, savings money tends to become blurred with cash budgeted for current expenses. All too often, it disappears, never to be found again.

FOUR WAYS TO FREEDOM

There are four combat techniques for keeping money away from those magnetic, free-spending fingers that, for most people, become outrageously overdeveloped during adolescence and never truly get cured.

Starting with the most time-consuming and moving to the easiest, the methods are:

- Physically shuffling funds from one account to another each time bills are paid and accounts are settled

- Arranging for direct deductions by an employer
- Arranging for automatic transfer from a bank account
- Putting every extra penny into a house in the form of big mortgage payments

THE HANDS-ON MONEY-HANDLER

For people who have tremendous self-control and who like to have a tactile relationship with their own money, the old-fashioned method of writing a check each month to one or several types of savings accounts works just fine.

The method isn't very complicated. Did your grandmother or an elderly aunt use a similar system for household accounts? With a collection of coin purses or battered brown envelopes, she would put her church tithe in one, coins for the paper carrier in another, and grocery money in a third, on down the line until the obligations were taken care of. And with luck, there would be something left over for the cookie jar.

MORE MODERN THAN AUNT MILLIE

Today's savers may utilize a more sophisticated ledger system, but the concept is identical: Physically put the money designated for one use over here and money designated for another use over there.

To implement certain tailor-made savings and investment programs, there may be no alternative to handling the transactions personally. For example, when setting up education funds for children, such as a Uniform Gift to Minors Act account, it would be best to design and execute the plan under the supervision of a tax accountant.

For many, there is a certain satisfaction in hands-on money management. Shopping for rates, recording transactions, computing earnings—especially for computer buffs—can be a hobby in itself. But a large number of people lack either the self-control or the time to engage in this type of financial participation.

PAY YOURSELF BEFORE YOU GET YOUR PAYCHECK

In today's busy world convenience has become a necessity, and for savings, nothing is more convenient than having funds automatically deducted from a paycheck or a bank account.

TOO GOOD TO PASS UP

Payroll deductions, made by your employer's own accountants and taken from your check, make even more sense when they have positive tax implications. About 85 percent of large and mid-size companies provide a profit-sharing, thrift or 401(k) plan. Contributions to 401(k) and 403(b) plans, which allow for deductions from pay *before* taxes are computed, are among the best tax shelters around. The advantages are even more apparent when the employer's matching contribution is considered.

Self-employed persons can also use Keogh accounts or other government-qualified pension plans to shelter some of their income for retirement.

The drawback here is that most of the plans have penalties for withdrawal before retirement, though some provisions are made for hardship withdrawal. More about 401(k)s, Keoghs and other tax-advantaged savings plans in Chapter 9.

SHELTERING CHILD CARE

Some employers also offer a special tax advantaged saving plan intended to pay for child care, elder care, and other tax-deductible expenses for care of dependent family members. While these programs are convenient and offer several tax benefits, they do require careful planning in order to receive the maximum benefit. Any money remaining in the account at the end of the year reverts to the employer.

DOING IT FOR UNCLE SAM

Many savers view U.S. Savings bonds as a quaint holdover from World War II. But several years ago the Treasury Department modernized the savings bond, giving it a more competitive, variable interest rate. Certain companies, especially those with many government contracts, still encourage workers to participate in the savings bond drive.

They have numerous advantages, especially for people who are saving money for educational purposes. The money to pay for the bonds—the amount can be as little as $50 per withdrawal period—"disappears" from paychecks automatically, before there is a chance to spend it elsewhere. Most people who use this savings method find that after several months they adjust to having a little less money in the pay envelope. And then when the bond arrives, it seems more like a bonus than a bother.

The catch to savings bonds, however, is that they must be held for at least five years to earn their full interest. For employees who might have been pressured into buying savings bonds that they don't want, it's possible to cash the bonds in immediately and transfer the money to another type of saving. However, in such a case a comparison of rates should be made to be certain that cashing in the bond is the best strategy.

More about savings bonds appears in Chapter 14 on government securities.

ELECTRONIC TRANSFER

Many companies allow employees to directly deposit part or all of a paycheck into a bank or credit union account. This can be especially convenient for couples who intend to save all of one spouse's paycheck to make a major purchase of some kind.

In fact, automatic check deposit is, for most people, simply a convenience. But bank accounts themselves can play an active role in a savings strategy.

CORPORATE COOPERATION

Most financial institutions will arrange for an automatic transfer of funds from a transactional account to a money market account, a savings account, or one of the hybrid savings vehicles that financial institutions started inventing in the mid 1980s when deregulation of financial services really took hold.

In addition, mutual funds, insurance companies, and brokerage houses often will set up automatic withdrawal of funds, to be applied to savings accounts, insurance premiums, or investments.

CASH MANAGEMENT MADE EASY

Individuals with a relatively high net worth also can utilize a cash management account at brokerage houses. Almost every brokerage, from discounters to full-service providers, offers CMAs.

The minimum deposit required to open a CMA varies from one brokerage to another, and in some cases it can be quite high. But for busy people who want active management of their money, the diversity of the account offers many advantages. More about CMAs later.

CLEVER COMBINATION

Any one of these strategies can be used on its own, or, as is more common, two or more can be used in combination to put together an entire bill-paying, money management, and savings package.

Kevin D. is an inventive saver who combined several savings alternatives to create a master plan that works, and that provokes a minimum amount of stress and pain for him. It also has cost him practically nothing in management fees.

First of all, Kevin participates in his employer's 401(k) savings and retirement plan. Through this employee benefit, his company matches up to 40 percent of his savings contribution. With Kevin's contribution of 10 percent of his gross salary (he could contribute more if he chose to) and the employer's matching fund, Kevin automatically deposits pre-tax dollars each month toward his long-term saving.

Where else could he get a tax deferral plus a 40 percent return on his investment? And best of all, the 401(k), on its own, meets Kevin's retirement savings goal.

Kevin's company also encourages employees to participate in a U.S. savings bond program. A small amount is withheld from each paycheck, and quarterly, a savings bond arrives in the mail at Kevin's house. The tax on interest earnings on the bonds is deferred until the bonds are redeemed. If the money from the bonds is spent for a student's college expenses, as Kevin intends to do, they will receive even more favorable tax treatment.

More information on saving for higher education for children is presented in Chapter 10.

Finally, Kevin uses his employee federal credit union for banking and short-term savings. The federally insured credit union offers an interest-bearing checking account, a savings account and certificates of deposit. His paycheck is automatically deposited into his credit union account; from that, a designated amount goes into his savings account each month.

ALL THIS AND DIVIDENDS TOO

Kevin's credit union allows transactions by telephone, so he is able to move money easily from one account to another.

To maximize his interest earnings and have fairly good access to funds, Kevin keeps three CDs with alternating maturities. And though his passbook savings account pays the usual 5 percent interest, the credit union is profitable; so each year it distributes "dividends" based on the number of "shares" held by members in their passbook accounts.

As the result of some simple planning, all Kevin has to do to track his finances is reconcile his paycheck stubs and credit union payments and keep track of his savings bonds and CDs. And at the end of the year, much of his tax work is already done, since the bulk of the information he needs appears on two documents, his year-end credit union statement and his final paycheck stub for the year.

Kevin owns a home, and makes monthly payments and takes tax deductions for interest paid on the mortgage. It is the place in which he intends to reside throughout his life. While he considers it a good investment, it's not an investment he plans to cash in.

SIZZLING SHELTERS

Home ownership, for most Americans, has been more than a matter of a place to live. It is a matter of status. For a guaranteed ticket to the middle class, a mortgage has been de rigueur. The American dream would be incomplete without it. But for many people, it is also seen as their foremost investment.

The practice of using a house as an investment vehicle is very common in California, New York City, and other high-growth regions where real estate prices have escalated faster than the inflation rate. In fact, in many states, for the past 30 years homebuyers could expect to make money on their homes if kept for any length of time before being resold.

Since 1970, the national median price of a new single-family house has nearly quintupled, from $23,400 to $114,000 in 1988. Resale prices have kept pace too. In Philadelphia, the prices of previously owned homes have climbed 44 percent, from $74,000 to $106,500.

In one Southern California beach town in 1988, home prices escalated at the rate of 3 percent per month. Only the most precarious investments offer more than 30 percent annual appreciation, and usually gains at this rate are not predictable—they just happen one day. Home ownership, generally, offers more predictability than other investments.

ADVANTAGES OF OWNERSHIP

Except in extremely depressed regions of the country where home prices sometimes either stagnate or fall rather than progress, a home traditionally has had two advantages:

- The value of the home and improvements to it keep up with inflation. If necessary, a house can be sold 5, 10, or 30 years after purchase, and the proceeds have (at least) the same purchase value as the original investment.
- The interest paid on the mortgages is tax-deductible, meaning that the homebuyer gets to use more of his or her paycheck for building an estate, rather than sending the money to Washington.

THE BOOM IS NO LONGER SONIC

However, demographers say that the time has ended when homebuyers could gamble with a mortgage and almost assuredly win. If U.S. League of Savings Institutions chief economist James Christian reads it right, in the decade ahead housing prices nationally will climb by only a modest 5 percent to 7 percent a year. When forecasts for annual inflation of 5 percent are factored in, that means that home prices will be essentially flat. While those who already own homes won't lose money on their purchases, potential buyers, who have seen house prices race ahead of their capability to buy, will get a break.

In part, the expected flattening of home prices is caused by the aging of the baby boomers. Demand will cool off, since many of those born between 1946 and 1964 will already have purchased homes. In the two decades following the post-war baby boom, about one million fewer children were born. As these children reach adulthood, they will put less pressure on the housing supply. In the mid 1980s, the birthrate started climbing again, but those kids won't be ready to buy homes until approximately the year 2010.

THE TAX TOLL

The 1986 tax cuts took their toll on home ownership as well. When Congress cut the top rate from 50 to 33 percent, the home-mortgage interest deduction became worth substantially less. When the top rate was 50 percent, spending $10,000 on mortgage interest meant paying only $5,000 after taxes. Now $10,000 in mortgage interest is worth only $3,300 to those who pay the maximum tax.

NO MORE SPRINGBOARD

So playing "house leapfrog"—buying a house, living in it as the price escalates, then selling and using the profits to trade up—will become a practice limited to certain high-growth and high-end neighborhoods. As the baby boomers get older and richer, they may try to outbid each other for the most desirable homes in the best locations. Then, say some real estate specialists, the homes left behind will be offered to a dwindling list of prospects.

LOAN COLLATERAL

Ever since Congress began phasing out consumer interest as a tax write-off, financial institutions have been advertising home equity loans as the best way to get credit and at the same time obtain tax relief from the interest payments.

However, there are two reasons to approach home equity loans tentatively:

- This is your home, after all. It would be foolish to risk the family's primary source of physical and emotional security for any use that does not also add substantially to their well-being. A loan to add bedrooms and bathrooms, for example, has merit, as the addition provides comfort and probably will add to the value of the house. A second mortgage loan to expand a booming business has worked well for many people, but the borrower should look closely at the potential for business failure. It would be doubly sad to have a business collapse, and then lose a home as well.
- The true cost of a home equity loan may be more than you think. In addition to interest payments, a second mortgage (also called a second trust deed in some states) involves appraisal and recording fees, lenders' points can be added in, and in some states a mortgage tax is connected with home equity loans. The cost of the loan must outweigh the tax and other advantages.

HOME STILL A HAVEN

Putting everything into the house still has a certain psychological appeal, it still holds tax advantages for some savers, and it remains the safest hedge against inflation. For all of these reasons, home ownership will generally be a solid part of a plan to accumulate wealth. But getting rich by buying and selling houses may not be the sure-fire financial tactic it once was.

RETIREMENT REVENUES

There are as many ways to save as there are savers. But without a specific strategy for putting money into banks or bonds or even an old sock, there wouldn't be any savers. And without savings, there wouldn't be as many financially independent, fun-loving senior citizens as there are. The retirement years, though longer and healthier than ever, otherwise could well be spent pinching pennies and praising the past.

Rescuing Hidden Cash

The following suggestions will help savers identify places to find more money to save.

• Refinance an expensive mortgage. Remember, however, that the new interest rate must be low enough to compensate for closing fees and other financing costs.

• Review consumer loans. For instance, if you are paying 12 percent interest on a car loan and have sufficient money in your intermediate-term savings account, but that account is paying only 7 percent, it certainly would be worth paying off the loan.

• Analyze your insurance coverage. Are your auto rates the best available to you? Are you entitled to special rates for non-smokers? You may be able to trim $200 or more from a $1,000 auto insurance premium by increasing the collision deductible from $100 to $500. If a disability policy begins paying benefits 30 days after a disability, changing to a 90-day waiting period could cut a premium from nearly $1,400 to just over $500. A study of life insurance from time to time also can pay off. New actuarial tables may have lowered costs, in some cases. And as time goes on and children leave the nest, some heads of household need less life insurance.

• If you pay off your credit cards each month, look for a card that has no annual fee. This can lop from

$20 to $50 per year from credit costs. And you probably need only one major credit card. No use paying the annual fee on more. If you're still paying off large balances, shop for a card or consumer loan with a low interest rate charge. The federal tax deduction for installment loan interest began to be phased out by the Tax Reform Act of 1986, and was to completely gone by 1990.

• Always maintain minimum deposits in a checking account, and shop for an interest-bearing account with the most convenient features available.

• Don't accumulate idle cash. Regularly sweep any excess money from a checking account into a savings account with a higher rate of return. Don't delay depositing paychecks, dividend checks, or any others that you receive. Collecting interest on an insured account is the easiest, most worry-free way to earn money that exists.

• Don't prepay bills. Check the due dates and pay only early enough to be certain to avoid late penalties. Keep the money in your own interest-earning checking account as long as possible.

• Do not over-withhold income tax deductions. The government does not return your taxes with interest. It uses the money interest-free, and you get nothing. The ideal is that when taxes come due, there is nothing more to pay and nothing to be returned. But perfect balance is difficult to achieve. In reality, a rebate of only a few hundred dollars is close enough.

• Encourage children to earn some of their own spending money, and even help them. Young children can collect aluminum cans, glass bottles, and newspapers for recycling. George L. made recycling expeditions family outings with his two young sons each Saturday. They took long walks at the beach, on country roads, and at a nearby hang-gliding field. The recyclable refuse they collected was turned in at a local center, and the kids got to keep the money. Sometimes the kids donated their earnings to a school or church project, and one year at Christmas they gave the money to the Salvation Army for a Yule dinner for the homeless. The amount of money involved wasn't much, but the kids felt good making these choices with something that was their own. And—maybe most important of all—they enjoyed the time dad spent with them.

• Check with your state or any other state where you have lived for unclaimed money in your name that may be lying in a government vault, just waiting for you to speak up. These funds accumulate from old bank accounts, forgotten tax returns, or abandoned utility deposits, and such. Most state governments have an unclaimed-property section, usually located at the state capitol. Beware of companies offering to do this search on your behalf. Their fees are likely to eat up most of any newly discovered cache.

CHAPTER 6

Saving for Retirement

"Ready Money is Aladdin's Lamp."

GEORGE GORDON, LORD BYRON, *Don Juan*

Probably no life event evokes as much ambivalence as the prospect of retirement. On one hand is the long-awaited freedom, either from work or to change to activities of one's own choosing. On the other hand, there is the uncertainty over financial comfort, even financial survival.

And of course, some people just want to keep on working. Having a job has been a pleasurable part of their lives; they fear that they may feel useless; they simply aren't ready to stop working.

THE RETIREMENT CROWD BECOMES A MOB

But for almost all of us, retirement will be a reality some day, and it is a time for which preparation must be made. Consider these facts:

- There are already 41,000 people 100 years of age or older.

- Two-thirds of all Americans live past 65, and 30 percent past 80.
- Average life expectancy for someone born this year is almost 75, and by the year 2000, life expectancy will be about 80.

As they remain healthier and live longer, more and more Americans will spend nearly as much time in retirement as they did working.

EXEMPLARY PREPARATION

Just as we spend the first quarter of our lives making ready for adulthood and our working years, we need to spend at least some of our middle years thinking about and planning for a comfortable and carefree retirement.

It's never too soon or too late to initiate planning and saving for retirement. Any planning that is intelligently done, even if it is five or fewer years before the actual retirement date, helps smooth the way.

PICTURE THIS

Planning should begin with visualization, and approached in the way in which your human eye and mind collaborate to take in a panoramic view. The mind comprehends large images in steps. First, the big, overall picture is seen. Then, gradually the eye picks out predominant shapes, sizes and colors. Eventually, you become aware of more and more detail.

The difference for retirement planning is that this is a lovely scene that you will paint for yourself. Put anything in it that you would like, then figure out how to afford the things you see.

The further away retirement is, the less clear the details are to most of us. If retirement is years and years off, the details may be fuzzy. In time, they will emerge. But one

Figure 6-1   **Age Investors Started Saving for Retirement**

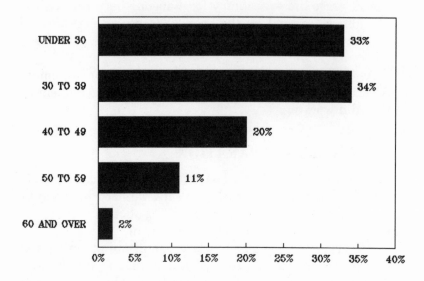

Courtesy of Fidelity Investments

thing most of us do know is that we want to be independent, both physically and fiscally.

Even though time could bring a change of taste, interest, or capability, retirement planning should begin as early as possible.

PICK A LIFESTYLE

Develop a general idea of where you want to live and what you want to do after you retire. Do you want to stay right where you are, near friends and family? Settle in a sunny retirement community in Florida or Arizona? Open a winery in California? Do you hope to travel? Play golf year-round? Raise Christmas trees? Write your autobiography?

Sure, you can change your mind and paint over a scenario, or pencil in details later. Revising relatively minor choices is not a problem. But it makes a big difference to planning that, for instance, you expect to stay in your home rather than to sell it and use the profits to relocate. You'll have more money if you work part-time. It takes capital to start a business. It matters to your budgeting whether you plan to go wandering abroad or simply want to stay put.

These decisions shape your savings program. They determine whether you can retire early or must wait until all your retirement benefits are at your disposal.

COMMON MISCALCULATION

Underestimating monetary needs is a common mistake in planning for retirement. Calculations are subject to two major pitfalls: inflation and life expectancy. Inflation is a creeping erosion that wears away at retirement income. It can transform what once seemed like a sizeable aggregate into an insignificant amount.

ESTIMATING INFLATION

Although consumer price increases have slowed considerably since the late 1970s, inflation is still expected to continue at an average rate of 4.5 to about 5 percent per year in the forseeable future. As for the more distant future, it's anybody's guess.

"If living costs rise at a moderate 5 percent," wrote *Money* magazine in 1989, "a pension payment of $1,000 a month when you were 60 would have only $277 of today's purchasing power when you hit 85."

Up ahead, Chapter 7 will help readers understand inflation, predict its course, and reckon with its impact.

TO A LONG LIFE

As for life expectancy, that's always a gamble. But statisticians do know that those who reach retirement age can expect to live beyond the typical life expectancy.

Ordinarily, someone born in 1930 could expect to live about 60 years. But if that person had survived childhood diseases, wars and automobile accidents in his or her early years, life span is greatly extended. Plans must be made for those extra years.

"At age 60, the median life expectancy is 20 years for a man," reported *Money* magazine, "and 25 for a woman. But those are only medians, and for that reason you really need to plan for 30 years or so."

STARTING EARLY

About 45 percent of men and 32 percent of women between ages 55 and 64 retire early. More and more early retirees are men—partly, it is surmised, because it is easier for men whose wives are employed to shorten their own working years. For those who hope to bail out of the work place ahead of schedule, a strategy is imperative, since early retirement implies the need for more years of income, and perhaps lower pension checks.

ASSESSING INCOME NEEDS

As a first step toward professional rest and relaxation, a future retiree should figure out how much retirement income is wanted. As a rule, retirees need about 70 percent of their pre-retirement wages to maintain their life styles. Stated another way, a retired person should plan to provide himself or herself with about 17 years of post-employment income.

Make a list of the things you plan to do—be it golfing, fishing, gardening, gourmet cooking, or crafts—then tot up the estimated cost. If you plan to travel, factor in more cash. Earmark $2,500 for one trip a year, and double that amount for an exotic escape.

Having made your wish list, estimate after-retirement expenses. While some people may choose to work periodically or part-time, that usually is an option only for the early part of the retirement years.

A TRIPOD

Retirement income, point out the experts, should be built on "three legs." They are:

- Social Security and other government pensions
- Employment pension plans
- Personal savings and investments

SOCIAL SECURITY

A very heated and emotional debate rages from time to time about the viability of the Social Security system into which

Figure 6-2 **Individual Investors' Savings and Investment Goals**

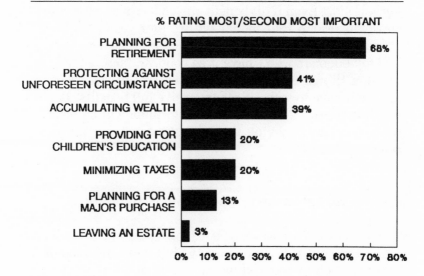

% RATING MOST/SECOND MOST IMPORTANT

Courtesy of Fidelity Investments

the majority of us have paid during most of our working lives. Whether an individual will be able to collect benefits 10, 30, or any number of years from now depends largely on how conscientiously Congress conserves the trust fund earmarked for this purpose.

No matter how congress performs, one thing seems certain. As the years progress, there will be further changes in Social Security benefits.

THE PAYBACK

While yesterday's and today's retirees collect a lot more from the system than they contributed, explained *Forbes* magazine, that will not be true for future beneficiaries. "A person who retired at 65 last year (1988), after 45 years of working and paying the maximum rate all his working days, would have paid into the system the equivalent of $38,000 in taxes (assuming 3 percent annual imputed interest)," *Forbes* said. "Even if his benefit stayed flat at $838 a month, he would recoup that money within four years. With cost of living increases, he will get it back even sooner."

Baby boomers won't have it so good. In fact, far from it. For one thing, anyone who turns 62 in the year 2000 or after will have to wait longer to receive full benefits. Beginning in the year 2000, the benefits formula will be restructured, gradually moving the full retirement age ahead to age 67.

Social Security Retirement Benefits

You can retire as early as 62, provided you are fully insured under Social Security, but your retirement benefit will be reduced permanently.

The normal retirement age today is 65. Starting in the year 2000, the age at which full benefits are payable will be increased in gradual steps until it reaches 67.

This will affect people born in 1938 and later. Reduced benefits will still be payable at 62, but the reduction will be larger than it is now. The following chart gives the Social Security normal retirement age by year of birth:

YEAR OF BIRTH	NORMAL RETIREMENT AGE[1]
1937 or earlier	65
1938	65 and 2 months
1939	65 and 4 months
1940	65 and 6 months
1941	65 and 8 months
1942	65 and 10 months
1943–1954	66
1955	66 and 2 months
1956	66 and 4 months
1957	66 and 6 months
1958	66 and 8 months
1959	66 and 10 months
1960 and later	67

[1]Normal retirement age is the earliest age at which unreduced retirement benefits can be received.

Source: Retirement, U.S. Department of Health and Human Services, Social Security Administration, SSA Publication No. 05-10035, January 1989, ICN 457500

"Peter Ferrara, senior fellow at the Cato Institute and author of several books on Social Security," said *Forbes*, "has formulated a model to forecast benefits for a baby boomer who entered the work force at 22 in 1980 and pays the maximum Social Security tax throughout his working life. Using constant 1980 dollars, Ferrara reckons this worker will pay the equivalent of $475,000 in Social Security taxes and imputed interest by the time he retires in 2023. With a benefit of $1,250 a month, it will take him 32 years to recoup the value of what he paid in."

The maximum amount of Social Security income that could be collected in 1989 was $899 per month. The average check was much smaller.

For those who retire before 65, the Social Security Administration uses as a basis what it calls the primary insurance amount, which is what you would have received had you waited until age 65, and reduces it by 5⁄9 of 1 percent for each month of retirement prior to age 65. For example, if you retire at age 63½ (18 months early), your monthly benefits would be cut back by 10 percent.

Social Security, by and large, is out of the hands of the saver and under the control of bureaucrats and elected officials. Laws and regulations change on a regular basis. Unless we participate in vigorous lobbying efforts, most of the more than 117 million people now covered by Social Security will be obliged simply to take what we get when the time arrives to retire.

What You Should Know About Social Security

- You must work and pay Social Security taxes for at least ten years to qualify for benefit checks. The longer you work under the system and the higher your earnings (up to a point), the larger your benefits.
- The earliest you can retire is age 62, but this carries a penalty. You'll receive only 80 percent of what you would have gotten if you had waited until 65. Wait to retire until age 70, and you'll get 30 percent more than if you'd stopped working at 65. And after your 70th birthday, the government sends checks, for a predetermined amount, whether you are retired or not.
- Social Security benefits are indexed. That is, they increase after your retirement begins in response to increases in the cost of living.
- Additional benefits are available for a spouse, and benefits continue to your spouse after your death. A spouse may choose to draw on his or her own account. Couples are allowed to choose the more advantageous of the two options.

- Medicare coverage is not accessible until age 65, except to the disabled. Medicare traditionally has covered only about 50 percent of all medical bills. Beginning in 1989, health care coverage under Medicare was expanded, but all taxpayers age 65 and over who were eligible for Social Security benefits were required to pay a new Annual Supplemental Medicare Premium based on taxable income.
- Periodically check Social Security regulations, since they will be changing in the year ahead.
- Check your own Social Security records, since the government sometimes makes mistakes. Fill out a request form available at the nearest Social Security office. You will get a comprehensive report showing the amount of covered wages you have earned since your first paycheck, along with other useful information. There is no charge for the service. For more information, contact your Social Security office. The Social Security Administration offers a booklet entitled "Retirement," that clearly explains the provisions of Social Security. It is available at most SSI offices.

Fortunately we have more control over private pension plans, and a lot more control over personal savings and investments.

PENSION PLANS

Thanks to Uncle Sam, there are retirement plans, many of them tax-sheltered, for almost every type of work situation:

- Traditional pension and profit-sharing programs for small, mid-sized, and large companies
- Employer-sponsored 401(k) savings programs
- Keogh and SEP plans for the self-employed

- Tax-sheltered annuity programs specifically for teachers and for those who work for nonprofit organizations
- Individual Retirement Accounts, although certain individuals reap more benefits than others

These are all explained in the following pages.

THE BEST BREAK

The 401(k) plan is an employer-sponsored, self-directed program in which participation is voluntary. Also known as a "cash-or-deferred arrangement," a 401(k) permits a worker to contribute up to 25 percent of pay per year, within certain limits. The maxium investment is adjusted each year for inflation; in 1989, it was $7,627.

MATCHING BENEFIT

Management may or may not match part of that contribution. The matching formula can vary enormously from company to company, but typically it is 50 cents for every dollar put in by the employee.

On top of this, the employee's entire contribution can be excluded from taxable income (though Social Security taxes must be paid). Earnings in this salary-reduction program compound tax-free until withdrawn.

DISADVANTAGES

The catch to a 401(k) and most other tax-sheltered retirement plans is that the savings may be tied up for a long time. Unless you become disabled or leave your job, you cannot withdraw 401(k) funds until you retire. Even if you leave a job, 401(k) funds must be rolled over into another retirement-type account.

Some hardship withdrawals are allowed for buying a house, financing education, or to meet certain crises, but in

---

Table 6–1
Computing 401(k) Account Growth

The numbers in this table assume that an employee contributes 5 percent of pay regularly, that the employer matches those contributions 50 percent (50 cents per $1 contributed) and that the investment grows an average of 5 percent each year.

Annual Income	Years in Plan				
	5	10	20	30	35
$20,000	$ 8,500	$19,300	$ 51,000	$102,000	$139,000
30,000	12,700	29,000	76,000	153,000	208,000
40,000	17,000	38,700	102,000	204,000	278,000
50,000	21,200	48,300	127,000	255,000	347,000
60,000	25,500	58,000	152,000	306,000	416,000

1987 rules for withdrawal were tightened considerably. Withdrawals are subject to any income tax owed and, under some circumstances, a 10 percent penalty tax.

For this reason, a worker should decide carefully how much to contribute to such a plan. To make the best of the tax break, the maximum contribution is preferable. But if there is a chance that you must have some of the money later, make a smaller contribution. No matter what, it would be foolish not to participate in a 401(k) if it is available to you. The amount contributed, fortunately, can be increased or decreased at certain specified intervals.

CASHING IN

At retirement time, lump-sum withdrawals from a 401(k) are eligible for income averaging or for rollover into an Individual Retirement Account.

YOU'RE IN CHARGE

A self-directed program means that the employee can decide how his or her contribution will be invested. Usually the choices include stock, bond, money market, guaranteed, or balanced funds managed by an outside firm. At regular intervals, customarily four times each year, the employee has the option of switching funds.

However, requests for changes don't mean an immediate transfer of funds. The modifications usually are made at a specific time, perhaps the first day of each quarter. A large number of 401(k) members discovered this fact after the October 1987 stock market crisis. They'd asked to be switched out of a stock fund, but learned later that the change had not yet taken place before the crash.

WIDEN THE BASE

Because of the fiduciary responsibility placed on pension fund managers, usually 401(k) stock funds are conservatively run and offer relative safety for the investor. Nevertheless, as with most other investment plans, it is wise to diversify a 401(k).

Because of the long-term nature of retirement investments, and the professional management built into the system, guidelines here are somewhat more flexible than with accounts we handle on our own.

While in the long run, stocks tend to outperform other investments, the risk of an abrupt decline is greater. A participant with plans to retire could quickly become low on funds in the face of a major market decline. If a stock fund is used for a retirement account, it should only be one that follows a very conservative, long-term philosophy.

If a company 401(k) plan allows for dividing investments into sectors, the safest tactic is to put one portion into long-term bonds, one part into a money market fund, and another into a guaranteed account. With this amount of diversification, it then would be acceptable to put one-fourth of the money into a blue chip stock fund. During a rising economy, it is safe to place a greater portion of the fund in blue chip stocks. In a declining economy, a larger amount should be allocated to bonds and money market funds.

These investment principles can also apply to other self-directed pension plans.

KEOGHS

Keoghs are tax-qualified retirement plans for doctors, dentists, lawyers, or other self-employed individuals and their employees. The Keogh is so-called for the congressman who sponsored the original legislation setting up the plan. Since the passage of the Tax Equity and Fiscal Responsibility Act there has been virtually no difference between corporate and non-corporate plans.

Incidentally, if *any* of your income derives from self-employment, even part-time, you may be eligible for a Keogh. This could be an excellent option for those who are dissatisfied with their employer's retirement plan. A tax accountant or pension consultant can offer advice on the best type of plan to set up and how it should be run. A Keogh can be established at a discount brokerage, allowing the participant to select from a wide array of investments.

SIMPLIFIED EMPLOYEE PENSIONS

SEPs, authorized by Congress in 1978 to allow self-employed workers to more easily provide themselves with tax deductions and pension benefits, are like Keoghs in many respects. People with no employees, or entrepreneurs who have full-time or part-time income from freelancing, consulting, or similar enterprises will find SEPs convenient.

With a SEP, you can make a tax-deductible deposit each year of up to 13.043 percent of your self-employment income, with a maximum contribution of $30,000. That money can be invested with a depository institution, mutual fund, brokerage, or most other types of investment sponsors.

Many of the same restrictions that apply to Keogh and IRA withdrawals pertain to SEPs as well. Any employee who has worked for you at least three out of the last five calendar years and who is at least 21 years of age must be offered the plan, and receive parity with the boss. Even part-time workers are included, as long as they meet the other guidelines, work a minimum of one day during the year, and have earned at least $300.

RUDIMENTARY REGULATIONS

While the IRS deadline for setting up a SEP is the same as the tax filing deadline (April 15 unless that day falls on a weekend), a Keogh must be established by December 31 of the tax year. So you can create a SEP during that last-minute scramble for tax deductions.

Rules regarding lump-sum distributions of SEPs differ from Keoghs, in that they do not qualify for income averaging, a tax-saving trick. The IRS offers publications spelling out the rules for SEPs, Keoghs, and other qualified retirement plans.

The paperwork for setting up a SEP is fairly simple, but to be sure the plan is best for both the employer and employee, an accountant or pension expert should be consulted.

PARTICIPATING IN PROFITS

A profit-sharing plan allows the employer to allocate a percentage of the corporation's profits to a pension plan. There are a number of formulas for determining how the profits will be determined and distributed. These plans, like 401(k) plans and Keoghs, are designed to encourage employees to be as productive as possible, since the company's profits directly affect their well-being.

Most employees are 100 percent vested in stock option plans from the beginning, and though withdrawals before retirement may be allowed, usually limitations are imposed.

REGULAR PENSION PLANS

Most of the plans described above are defined *contribution* programs, meaning that they are voluntary; a worker may choose to not participate. Defined *benefit* plans, those provided by an employer as a benefit, are not voluntary. Employers are not required to offer a defined-benefit plan, but 79 percent of large companies and 16 percent of companies with fewer than 500 employees do so.

Benefits are calculated by a formula taking into consideration the years worked and the salary level.

VESTING

In the past, most workers had to be employed by a company for ten years before becoming vested, or entitled to collect benefits. That changed with the 1986 Tax Reform Act.

Now the vesting period is reduced to five years, or to partial vesting after three years with full vesting after seven. The years a person has already worked for the present employer count. The vesting rules apply to both contributory and non-contributory pension plans, by the way.

THE REVERSION HAZARD

One threat to pension has been "pension reversion," a practice by which a company terminates an over-funded employees defined-benefit pension plan, then buys annuities to cover its vested workers and retirees, keeping the rest of the money. This can work to the detriment of employees.

"Employees are denied future expected benefits from increases in the value of the funds," reported *Changing Times* magazine in 1989, "and those already retired have to do without increases in pensions entirely. About two million people have been members of such terminated plans, estimates the Pension Benefit Guaranty Corp."

Early in 1989 the Treasury Department declared a six-month halt to the practice. Organizations for retired people vowed to fight for a permanent halt, while business lobbies argued that reversions are their right, since the money belongs to companies, not to their workers and retirees.

TEACHER'S PET

Teachers and employees of certain nonprofit organizations generally are covered by Social Security and probably by regular state or other pension plans. Additionally, they qualify for special tax-sheltered annuities that allow sheltering of up to 20 percent of gross income, to a maximum of $9,500 per year. The teacher's TSA is a liberal annuity, with favorable provisions for borrowing before retirement and for rollovers at retirement.

IRAs STILL AN OPTION

IRAs are odd ducks in that they don't require any particular kind of employment, only that a person have earned income. In some cases they can be an alternative to a retirement plan; in others a supplement. In most situations, however, the individual figures out eligibility and sets up his or her own account.

The glory days of the IRA started in 1982 when tax law changes permitted any employed person under the age of 70½ to contribute up to $2,000 to an IRA annually. The IRA amount could then be deducted from gross income for the year. By the time the laws changed in 1986, Americans were putting away about $36 billion a year in the retirement accounts.

The amended IRA rules created two classes of workers for IRA purposes: those who are covered by employer pension plans and those who are not. Those not under an employer plan still may take a full deduction on their IRA contributions of up to $2,000 a year, regardless of how much they earn.

For those covered by a company pension plan, the maximum allowable contribution remains $2,000, but deductibility rules depend on the level of adjusted gross income, as shown Table 6–2.

While a nondeductible IRA produces no immediate tax saving, the interest earned on the contribution will accumulate tax-free until funds are withdrawn.

IRA money can be invested in stocks, mutual funds, bonds, zero-coupon Treasury issues, FDIC-insured money market accounts, and many other investments. However, Certificates of deposit perhaps are the most common IRA vehicle. Collectibles, real estate, and most precious metals cannot be held in an IRA.

Withdrawals without penalty are permissible at age 59½. But withdrawals *must* begin no later than April 1 of the year the IRA holder reaches age 70½.

Withdrawal need not be in a lump sum, however. The Internal Revenue Service provides guidelines for spreading withdrawals out over an expected lifetime.

IRAs are still an excellent option for those who can deduct the contribution from gross income for tax purposes.

Table 6–2
IRA Deductibility Rules
(For individuals covered by company pension plans)

If adjusted gross income is:		A $2,000 contribution is:
Joint Filing	Single Filing	
Under $40,000	Under $25,000	Fully deductible
$40,000 to $50,000	$25,000 to $35,000	Partially deductible
Over $50,000	Over $35,000	Nondeductible

If you are able to fund only a nondeductible IRA, compare possible IRA earnings with those available from other tax-advantaged investments. The money may be better off in a tax-free municipal bond or muni bond unit trust; here, not only will the money be available if necessary before retirement, but also the paperwork will be easier.

STAY ALERT FOR RULE CHANGES

Like Social Security and everything else over which government legislators have dominion, pension plan and IRA laws are subject to continual modification. Lawmakers and others are always trying to make a good thing better, prevent abuse, or eke out a little more dough for the tax coffers. As retirement draws near, it is worthwhile to check with the pension planner in your company's human resource division or some other financial adviser to be sure you understand all your benefits and how they will work together. Most large companies offer retirement planning counseling for employees.

FEW PENSION PLAN PARTICIPANTS

Unfortunately, though the actual number of Americans participating in company-sponsored pension plans has been increasing as more people have entered the work force, the percentages of workers in the plans has been slowly but steadily declining since the late 1970s. In 1986, 51.2 percent, only slightly more than half, of all workers had private pension coverage. This troubling statistic means one thing: Building a retirement nest egg with personal savings is absolutely essential for a very large number of people.

PERSONAL SAVINGS

When Social Security and pension plans are insufficient to meet retirement living expenses, personal savings can come

Table 6-3
Personal Savings Monthly Withdrawal Chart

Beginning Savings	10 Yrs.	Withdraw these amounts for the cash to last: 15 Yrs.	20 Yrs.	25 Yrs.	Withdraw this amount to keep original sum whole
$ 10,000	$ 116	$ 89	$ 77	$ 70	$ 59
20,000	232	179	155	141	118
30,000	348	269	232	212	179
40,000	464	359	310	282	237
50,000	580	448	386	352	285
60,000	696	538	464	424	360
80,000	928	718	620	564	467
100,000	1160	896	772	704	585

to the rescue. And except for the amount needed for your financial cushion to protect against catastrophe, savings should be used at this time to make life more enjoyable.

Table 6-3 shows how much can be taken from a nest egg each month before depleting savings. The table assumes an interest rate of 7 percent per year, compounded quarterly, before income-tax considerations.

INSURANCE SAVING PRODUCTS

Two other savings devices, both insurance products, may be useful to the person saving for retirement: annuities and universal life insurance. These can have distinct advantages in planning retirement savings, and will be discussed in greater detail in Chapter 16.

OTHER SOURCES OF INCOME

Other wellsprings of retirement income are limited only by an individual's resourcefulness. Here are a few possibilities:

- Ownership in a company or some other asset may be sold before retirement, with financing terms that provide long-term income and perhaps an estate for heirs.
- A corporate executive may continue to serve as a consultant to or member of the board of directors of his or her company or other companies. Such executives collect director's fees, and at the same time are able to make use of their years of accumulated experience.
- A farm or other real estate may be leased out to provide income that will be able to grow as inflation pushes the cost of living higher.

INCOME VERSUS OUTFLOW

When potential and actual expenditures have been subtracted from income, you should have a pretty good idea whether your retirement plans, pensions, savings, and other sources of income will be adequate. And if they are not, there is no time better than the present to rectify the shortfall.

PART
3

The Technical Aspects of Saving

CHAPTER 7

Understanding Inflation

"It never will rain roses: when we want
To have more roses we must plant more trees."

GEORGE ELIOT, *The Spanish Gypsy*

Earlier chapters established that all Americans should be savers, for their own sakes as well as for the sake of their families. Then we figured out where savings funds would come from and to what use they eventually will be put.

Between spending and saving, a lot of territory must be covered. It is important to know the best place to store those accumulated dollars. Money market funds? Certificates of deposit? Zero-coupon bonds? Insurance products? They all can sound good, especially when promoted by a skilled salesperson.

But the truth is that there is no single, simple, permanent, *best* place to save. The "Best" is a constantly moving target, and the target is being relocated by economic conditions and your individual and unique needs. Inflation, interest rates, and taxes each influence our choices, and each wields its power in different ways.

"Whoa," you might be thinking. "I'm not a trained economist. How can I master subjects that even the experts struggle with? Isn't this heavy, heady stuff?"

John Kenneth Galbraith did describe economics as the "dismal science," but he never said that the fundamental concepts were impenetrable. Just as the layperson—in most circumstances—can tell the difference between a simple cold and pneumonia, between a bruised shin and a broken leg, so too can most of us learn to interpret economic symptoms.

Like the body, the economy also sends signals. Though the economy is massive and complex, it is somewhat cyclical, and it reacts in fairly predictable ways to certain events. After all, "the economy" is little more than the aggregate impact of what you and I and thousands of others are doing every day. One of the most important things we do is cope with inflation.

Though inflation is invisible except when reflected on price tags at department stores, at gasoline pumps, and in other charges, it holds enormous sway over our financial well-being.

We've all heard it said: "Oh-oh. Here comes inflation. Trouble ahead." Actually, inflation is almost always with us. Prices may fluctuate, but in the long run they generally rise, causing currency to be worth less over time.

Remember those catalogs from the 1920s or even the 1950s? People get a lot of laughs from seeing how little razor blades, underwear, and washing machines cost back then. Seldom do we sit around laughing at how *much* things used to cost. The goods we bought in the past tend to hold their value, even as they age. The antique Sears & Roebuck catalog is a keen reminder that inflation is ever with us.

DEFLATION IS NO GOOD EITHER

Most of us plan our financial lives with the expectation of some inflation; if it disappeared and we had deflation (a zero inflation rate is practically impossible to maintain), the economy would be in serious trouble. The houses, farms and factories we bought or built last year, or even years before, could be worth considerably less than we paid for

89

them. Property owners would be tempted simply to walk away from mortgages, and other loans because they would be paying more for the asset than they could get for selling it.

In that event, the banks would find themselves with a batch of defaulted loans. That would trigger a wave of bank failures and general business chaos. Unemployment would climb and the economy would spiral downward.

INFLATION OUT OF CONTROL

Despite that frightening specter of deflation, run-away inflation is by far a more common threat, and prices that are soaring—or that could do so at any moment—create a serious concern. With an understanding of what inflation is, and how it is caused and controlled, we have a better chance of predicting its course and adjusting savings strategies accordingly.

Most people remember the high inflation of the late 1970s and early 1980s. The 13 percent inflation rate of that recent era frightened people and disrupted the normal flow of the economy.

NATIONS IN CHAOS

But 13 percent was nothing when compared with the "hyperinflation" in Germany during the early 1920s. Prices rose one trillion percent in 22 months, until it cost 100 billion marks to mail a letter. America suffered its own hyperinflation after the Revolutionary War, when the purchasing power of the Continental dollar fell to a thousandth of its original value. Mexico, Israel, and several other countries have suffered annual inflation rates of 100 percent in recent years.

WHAT IS NORMAL INFLATION?

The preceding examples give an idea of how bad inflation can get. But what *should* the rate of inflation be? How much

Figure 7–1   **The Course of Inflation in the '80s**

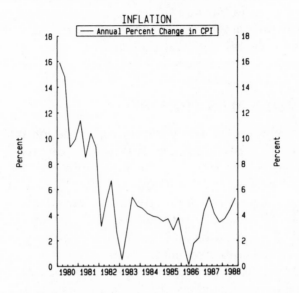

Source: *Credit Decisions* January 9, 1989

inflation can the U.S. economy withstand and still maintain its health?

THE FABULOUS '50S

During most of the 1950s and early 1960s, the annual inflation rate was less than 2 percent, and sometimes as low as 1 percent. People began to think inflation had been vanquished permanently. But as is inevitably the case, inflation showed all the tenacity of crabgrass.

"What had cost $1 to buy in 1970 cost $2.47 in 1980," wrote Robert M. Gardiner in *The Dean Witter Guide to Personal Investing.* "But this was not bad news for everybody. People who had bought $30,000 homes in 1965 with 6 percent mortgages found that their houses were now worth

91

$100,000 and that the monthly mortgage payments they had worried so much about being able to afford back in 1965 now looked like bus fare."

In the early stages of rising inflation, people usually don't complain. Wages rise, and though costs creep up too, the increases seem moderate.

THE FED HOLDS THE LINE

Historically, the economy tolerates an inflation rate of 2½ percent to 3½ percent per year. When the rate reaches 4 to 5 percent the Federal Reserve invariably gets concerned, and by 5 percent it takes definitive action. The Fed pushes interest rates higher in an attempt to encourage people to buy less, allowing prices to recede.

Actually, ascending and descending prices are a normal part of predictable economic cycles. If left alone, prices should decline. Even without Federal Reserve intervention, inflated prices should eventually decline as a result of normal market forces.

Investment writer Paul Erdman uses a classic classroom example to explain supply and demand and the cyclical nature of the economy.

"The pig cycle explains it best," he wrote in *Paul Erdman's Money Book*. "When the price of pork starts to rise, the farmers inevitably expand their operations to breed more pigs. Who wouldn't? Eighteen months later the little pigs that resulted are now big pigs: the supply of pork dramatically increases. The consequent excess supply results in falling prices. Prices fall so far that it costs the farmer more to feed the pigs than he's getting for them in the marketplace. So he stops breeding them. Eighteen months later there is a shortage of pigs. So pork prices start to rise again. Soon the prices exceed feed costs per pig. So on and on."

This is a simplistic example, of course, using only one variable factor. In the real world, millions of domestic and international factors are at work in our economy. That's what makes management of inflation by the government so difficult.

Traditionally, it takes the economy from three to ten years to work through a cycle, though many economists note that the highs and lows have become more extreme in recent years, and that the hills and valleys of the cycles themselves have been exaggerated.

NATURAL FORCES CAN BE ROUGH

Unfortunately, prices sometimes get very high before cooling off. And the correction occasionally goes too far the other way, causing a recession or even a depression. The Federal Reserve and government economists, in their attempts to modulate the economy, aim at flattening out its ups and downs, and keeping it on a smooth and steady path of growth.

WAGE/PRICE SPIRALS

Typically, rising inflation can be anticipated by one of two major signals: Either prices go up, or wages go up.

Prices may rise for any number of reasons, including a shortage of raw materials, an interruption in the supply because of a transportation catastrophe (an Alaskan oil spill, for example), or a crop-destroying drought. Workers then demand more money because they must pay higher prices for the goods they buy.

But wages, at times, become the engine pushing inflation. Especially at a time of full employment, wages can escalate first because of a shortage of qualified workers to fill jobs. Years ago, labor negotiations at coal mines and steel mills were major news stories, because increased wages in these big, primary industries could spur inflation throughout the economy. In these cases, increased employment costs forced companies to charge more for products or services, so salaries, rather than prices, led the way to inflation.

While unemployment figures offer a clue that inflation may be on the way (the lower the unemployment rate, the greater the prospects), the consumer price index is the most familiar tool for keeping track of inflation. The CPI regularly is reported in the news, and it's easy to understand.

YOU'RE THE "C" IN THE CPI

The CPI is a measure of the average change in prices over time of a fixed market basket of goods and services. It is based on prices of food, clothing, shelter, fuel, transportation fares, medical fees, and other items people need to buy day-to-day. The index measures price changes from a designated reference date—1967—which equals 100.0. The Labor Department actually sends agents out to fill in a list of prices at supermarkets, department stores, and similar places where consumers spend their money. The prices are compared month to month.

Changes in any one of the categories can move the CPI up or down. How much impact a rising or falling CPI will have on any one individual depends on where and how that person lives and in which categories the changes take place.

INDEX INGREDIENTS

Food and energy are not the largest segments of the CPI, but they are the most volatile components. Food and beverages account for 18 percent of the CPI market basket; housing 42 percent; energy 7.6 percent; and costs for health care 6 percent. Transportation fares and other miscellaneous expenditures make up the remainder.

ALL EYES ON OIL

Though energy costs represent only 7.6 percent of the CPI, oil prices are a key indicator of inflation because they have an impact on so many areas. And when the price of oil goes up, consumers still must buy a certain amount regardless; there are few substitutes for oil, despite efforts to develop nuclear and solar energy sources.

Remember the oil crisis of the 1970s and the inflation and rocketing interest rates that followed? One of the reasons inflation was so low in the 1980s is that OPEC, the oil-producing cartel, was in disarray, and thus oil prices remained low most of the decade.

The breakdown of the components of the CPI presented earlier in this chapter shows why homeowners tend to do better in times of rising costs. They've already purchased their homes, so mounting housing costs, which make up the lion's share of the CPI, mean less.

Savings and cash reserves, however, tend to be vulnerable to inflation, especially in its early stages, when interest rates on savings vehicles may have not yet gone up accordingly.

SAFEGUARDS FOR SAVERS

So a saver must know how to respond under each of the following circumstances:

- Inflation is under check.
- The inflationary cycle is just beginning.
- Disinflation (a declining rate of increase) is in force.

How a saver should cope with inflation has a lot to do with interest rates, which will be covered in more detail in the following chapter. But inflation and interest rates, as we have noted, are inextricably linked.

ON A BALANCING BEAM

When inflation is stable, savers can do nothing better than take advantage of the best rates of return available to them. Equilibrium, however, is always found somewhere on an

95

Figure 7–2   **The Inflation Spectrum**

Low Inflation----------------------Stability----------------------High Inflation

1% to 2%   2.5% to 4.5%   5% and above

Source: *Credit Decisions* January 9, 1989

---

ever-moving scale between very high and very low inflation rates.

If a saver should note that the inflation rate is uncommonly low, when only months before inflation had been a nagging national problem, probably there is a fair stretch of manageable inflation ahead. But when the stability has been maintained for a considerable amount of time, the best tactic is to anticipate rising interest rates in the foreseeable future.

If inflation has been accelerating and interest rates seem very high, a lower inflation rate can be anticipated once rates have peaked and inflation has been conquered.

Under most circumstances, a saver needs to be concerned less about where the inflation rate stands at the moment than with where it is headed.

TENTATIVE TIMES

In times of rising costs, most people save less and buy more *things*, because they know *things* will cost more in the future. They turn to gold, rare coins and stamps, antique cars or esoteric collectibles—it hasn't always mattered much what. If prices are rising, they buy tangible goods.

The problem with this strategy is the risk involved. Who would have thought that Kewpie and Barbie dolls would become collector's items? In contrast, some traditionally popular collectibles can suddenly become less fashionable and lose value. And amateurs shouldn't try to dabble in assets such as investment-grade diamonds or philatelic stamps. One needs to develop a significant level of expertise to do well with such highly sophisticated investments as these.

Even gold, a traditional inflation-hedging commodity in which many people hold an almost religious faith, does not always behave predictably. Just ask those people who bought gold in 1980 at $850 an ounce. Since the early 1980s, gold declined to lows well below $400 per ounce, and during the 80s, gold prices failed to go up when interest rates did, or in response to the threat of inflation.

A HOUSE WITH A HEDGE

However, few investors have gone wrong buying properly priced real estate in a good neighborhood during episodes of rising prices. Even in times of relative low or moderate inflation, houses and other real estate tend to be the best defense against the erosion of value.

In 1989, for instance, *Money* magazine was predicting a 4.5 to 5 percent inflation rate. At the same time, the publication expected home prices to increase about 5.4 percent.

If a savings goal has been to purchase a house, the prime time to buy is when inflation has been stable for an extended period or is just beginning to intensify. Conversely, when inflation is near a peak and interest rates still are rising, hold off. Once high interest rates have taken their toll, house prices and interest rates probably will back down somewhat. At the very least, prices will stabilize, and you won't be caught in the trap of chasing crazily rising prices. It is a time to have patience.

While rates are high, collect those high rates on your savings and have faith that what goes around comes around. Prices eventually will flatten and interest rates will come down.

AN INFLATIONARY LIFT

Part of the reason real estate serves its owners well in inflationary episodes is that it is usually bought on credit. The property is purchased at a specific price, then paid for in less valuable dollars as prices escalate.

"Real estate investments like this were especially profitable because of leverage," explained Robert Gardiner. "If you buy a $100,000 condominium for $100,000 cash and sell it a year later for $120,000 you have made 20 percent on your money. Not bad. But what if you buy a $100,000 condominium for $20,000 down and take out a mortgage to pay for the rest? If you sell the unit a year later for $120,000, you have made $20,000 on an actual cash investment of only $20,000. So you have made 100 percent of your money (less carrying charges). This is leverage in action. It made a lot of money for a lot of people."

That isn't to say nobody has ever lost money in real estate or when using leverage. Leverage, Gardiner pointed out, works both ways. "Just as it enables investors to make 100 percent on their money in a single year when property values are racing up," he wrote, "so does it enable them to lose 100 percent of their money in a single year when property values come down."

The hapless ones are those who bought at the peak of the inflation/interest rate cycle; who bought in markets that were over-priced; or who were the unlucky victims when economic disaster hit. There was a lot of cheap real estate on the Denver and Dallas markets in the 1980s after the oil industry went bust. Proper timing, in buying real property, is essential.

SAVERS CAN PROSPER

As long as inflation doesn't get completely out of hand and turn into hyperinflation, most savers can find ways to manage in inflationary times, especially if they aren't overly encumbered with variable-rate or high fixed-rate loans. The deregulation of the financial markets has meant that interest rates on money market accounts and certificates of deposit are much more responsive to inflationary pressures and to attempts by the Federal Reserve to curb inflation.

Because inflation often is followed by rising interest rates, many savers actually emerge from these cycles with enhanced earnings on their reserve accounts.

SAFE FROM THE CPI

Inflation universally is seen to be the foe of senior citizens, those who live on fixed incomes. But it ain't necessarily so.

One retired grocery store owner explained that he was incensed that the government was sweetening its cost-of-living increases to Social Security recipients. It was the early 1980s, when inflation had risen to terrible levels. He felt that boosting pension payments would only make inflation worse, in effect raising the wages for a significant part of the population. This, he felt, would damage the economy further.

"Most of us don't need it," he argued. "A lot of us older people own our homes. Housing isn't going up for us. We don't buy a lot of clothes or other things. I sure don't buy as many groceries as I used to."

This man happened to live in a warm climate and didn't need heating oil to survive the winter. Since he used public transportation, he was luckier than most. But he wasn't alone in feeling that inflation isn't as bad for retirees as most economists think it is.

TRAUMATIZED T-BILLS

When inflation had abated toward the mid-1980s and interest rates had come down to single digits, an elderly woman complained at a senior citizen's forum about low rates. "I want to know what the government is going to do about these low interest rates," she demanded. "My Treasury Bills aren't bringing the income they once did and I'm finding it very difficult to get along."

She was among the fortunate who supplemented her pension checks with a sizable amount of savings. She had become accustomed to living well on outrageous interest rates, without realizing that interest rates are an important economic tool. The art of managing savings depends on an understanding of interest rates.

CHAPTER 8

Understanding
Interest Rates

*"Money is the seed of money,
and the first guinea is sometimes more
difficult to acquire than the second million."*

JEAN-JACQUES ROUSSEAU

When we are borrowers, it's easy to remember what interest rates really represent: They are the cost we pay for using someone else's money. It's important for savers to remember that the reverse also is true; the interest we earn on our funds represents the fee a bank, the government, or any other entity is paying to borrow *our* money.

MONEY SUPPLY

Money, like all other commodities, is subject to the law of supply and demand. When there is a lot of money around, it is easy to acquire and the interest cost is low. When the demand rises or supply dries up, money becomes dear, and the cost—the rate of interest—goes up.

For the most part, the Federal Reserve Bank in the United States controls the supply of money and interest rates, though the Fed's grip isn't as tight as most people think.

"We don't move the markets," explained one Federal Reserve economist, "we only influence them."

COMPETITION FOR FUNDS

One force that can move the markets is big borrowers—government and industry. With their huge demand for money, they can eat up most of the available reserve.

"The position of the U.S. as a debtor nation," wrote Bob Black in a 1989 issue of his "Taking Stock" newsletter, "owing $400 billion and running a $155 billion deficit, 3.1 percent of GNP last years, serves to place government in competition with private industry for available funds, and puts further pressure on interest rates."

The most notable competitors for money are large corporations who finance their operations with a number of techniques, the most prevalent of which in recent years has been low-quality, high-yielding debt, so-called junk bonds.

"U.S. corporations have been substituting debt for equity for the past nine years," Black continued, "taking on $184 billion last year alone."

The leveraged buyout of RJR Nabisco by the investment firm of Kohlberg Kravis & Roberts in 1988, the largest LBO in history at the time it occurred, demonstrates why corporate debt levels had grown so huge. The $25 billion deal generated $20 billion in junk bonds, most of which were eagerly bought for those seeking lofty returns—such as high-yield bond mutual funds.

THE FED FIGHTS INFLATION

Corporations, when shopping for funds to borrow, keep close watch on the Fed, which has only one tool to manipulate the economy—interest rates. It is, however, a powerful tool.

When inflation is under control and the economy is doing well, rates usually are left to be set in the marketplace. But when inflation takes off, that's another matter.

RESTRICTING RESERVES

To help curb inflation, the Fed, the nation's central bank, pulls out reserves from the banking system, thus raising the key federal funds rate, which is the interest that banks charge each other for lending excess reserves. This rate also is known as the "overnight" rate, because banks frequently make very short-term loans to one another, from the close of one business day to the opening of the next, to keep federally mandated reserves at the proper levels.

THE DISCOUNT RATE

The Fed also sets the rate it charges for loans it makes directly to banks to cover reserves. This is the "discount" rate, and it provides a floor on interest rates, since banks set their interest rates a notch above the discount rate.

The expense banks pay for their own loans is an important cost of money. If the federal funds rate and discount rate are low, the banks can charge lower interest rates. But if upward pressure is kept on these rates long enough, it forces banks to boost the rates they charge their commercial and private borrowers.

FEDERAL FUNDS RATE

In tracking the direction of interest rates, the federal funds rate is the most sensitive indicator of the direction of interest rates, since it is set daily by the market. But of course for businesses and consumers, this is only a directional signal. It isn't the rate that is available to borrowers or savers.

103

REAL INTEREST RATES

The interest rates quoted in advertisements, in small print in the business sections of newspapers, and regularly in many general newspaper and magazine articles, are what the retail market is paying, but this is not the information that seasoned savers should use to gauge the status of the current rate of interest and the progress they are making in accumulating wealth.

The rate that financial institutions and other saving sources will pay for deposits is the "nominal" rate. What is important is the "real" rate of return.

"The real rate is the difference between the nominal (stated) interest rate of an investment and the current rate of inflation," explained Robert Gardiner in *The Dean Witter Guide to Personal Investing*. "If your money is in a bank account paying 5.5 percent, and the inflation rate is 5.5 percent, then your nominal interest rate is 5.5 percent, but your real interest rate is zero. Five-and-a-half minus five-and-a-half equals zero. The purchasing power of your money is not increasing at all."

MINIMUM EXPECTATIONS

Gardner added, "Historically, investors have expected a real rate of return of about 3 or 4 percent on safe investments. Short-term Treasury bills are about the safest investment around, so they generally end up selling for 3 to 4 percent above the current inflation rate."

In fact, say some financial advisers, if those individuals living off of their interest or investment earnings cannot survive on a 3 to 4 percent real rate of return, their capital pool is too small. They must resist the temptation to increase earnings by taking more risk. Rather, they need to enlarge the size of their savings or investment pool.

CORNERING ON THE CURVE

When shopping for the best rates, savers also need to be aware of the impact of time on their earnings. A yield curve best demonstrates how time and rates work together.

Under ordinary circumstances, rates rise with the length of time of the investment. A three-month certificate of deposit pays less than a one-year CD. The reason is rudimentary: If savers commit their money for more time, they take more risk (either of default by the lender or of missing a better rate somewhere else) and demand a greater return.

STANDARD CONFIGURATIONS

The most often-used yield curve provides a silhouette of Treasury securities with maturities ranging from three months to 30 years. Yield curves can assume several configurations:

- A positive yield curve bends upwards, with longer-term securities paying higher rates than short. This is considered the normal contour.
- A flat yield curve is exactly what it sounds like. There is little difference between long-term and short-term rates. A "hump" can pop up in the curve when only some short instruments pay higher rates than long-term securities.
- A negative or inverted yield curve occurs when short-term rates move higher than long-term rates. Total inversion is said to have arrived when the shortest rates, three-month Treasury Bills, exceed the longest rate, the 30-year bond.

YIELD VERSUS MATURITY

Not only does the yield curve offer clues as to the direction rates are headed, but professional investors also use it as a

Figure 8-1   **Yield Curve**

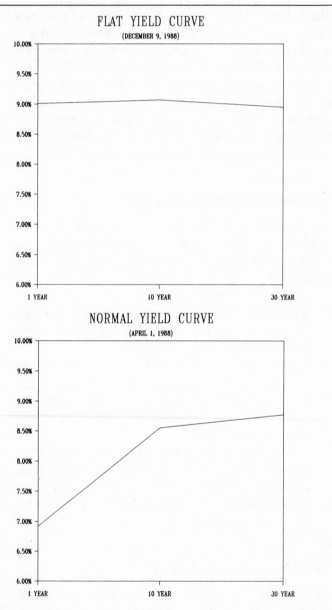

Courtesy of Dunham & Greer Investment Counsel

Figure 8–1 (continued)   **Yield Curve**

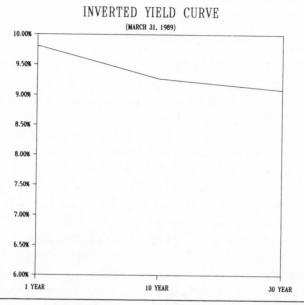

INVERTED YIELD CURVE
(MARCH 31, 1989)

Term	Flat Curve (12/9/88) % Yield	Normal Curve (4/1/88) % Yield	Inverted Curve (3/31/89) % Yield
1 Year	0.0901	0.0692	0.0981
10 Year	0.0907	0.0855	0.0927
30 Year	0.0895	0.0877	0.0909
Source:	Barron's 12/12/88 Issue	Barron's 4/4/88 Issue	Barron's 4/3/89 Issue

Courtesy of Dunham & Greer Investment Counsel

DUNHAM & GREER
SAN DIEGO, CALIFORNIA

tool for deciding where the highest yield for the least risk can be found.

WARNING BELLS

Alarms ring throughout the land when the curve flattens, and sirens really blare when it inverts. An inversion frequently develops when the Fed has handed out its strongest medicine for fighting inflation.

The inversion typically occurs at the top end of a business cycle and lasts for 10 to 12 months.

An inverted yield curve is believed harmful to the economy, because it indicates that long-term rates are considered by borrowers to be too low. They are not willing to commit to such low rates for an extended period of time, and turn to shorter maturities. The demand rises, then, for shorter-term money, and the cost of short-term funds rises accordingly. Savers, "stay short" under such circumstances because they believe interest rates will be going higher. They hope to be positioned to take advantage of higher future rates.

Without the stability provided by longer-term deposits and loans, interest rates become very volatile. Rates can move fast, and the movements can be more extreme in either direction than they are in normal circumstances.

Throughout the 20th century, an inverted yield curve nearly always has resulted in a recession, usually within 10 to 12 months. The exception was in 1966, when growth did slow but without a full-blown recession. A negative yield curve in 1980 ushered in the 1981–82 recession.

WRESTLING WITH A RECLINING YIELD

An inverted yield curve, according to most professional investors, shows that interest rates have not yet peaked. But savers can track certain signs to determine when and which way rates are turning.

When the yield curve became negative early in 1989, experts suggested that savers watch such indicators as the average maturity of money market mutual funds and the amount of cash in bond funds as clues as to what professional investors expected of interest rates. Short maturities and large cash positions would indicate that fund managers are making the most of short-term rates, but are poised to move long when appropriate. When those maturities extend and cash positions shrink, it is an indication that fund managers believe the curve will be bending toward a more normal arch.

Normalization can take two forms. Long-term rates will rise or short-term rates will decline. If rates on accounts with maturities of less than one year decline, it is an indication that interest rates have peaked. It is safe to lock in long-term rates. If short rates hold steady but long-term rates inch up, wait for a normal curve to return before committing to accounts of more than three years.

CLUES TO CORRECTION

The prices of oil and other commodities also are an early indicator of inflation and mounting rates, since they tend to cause these events, rather than result from them.

Auto sales react quickly to interest rate changes, with sales either improving as rates go lower or falling off as they ascend. Likewise, housing sales and new housing starts are reactive.

INTEREST RATE MARKERS

As mentioned earlier, a great many factors act as indicators for inflation and indicate the current drift in interest rates:

- The prime rate is perhaps the easiest indicator to monitor when watching for rate changes, because it is published in many daily newspapers, with changes in the prime covered even more widely. Note that, in reality, there is no single prime rate; each financial institution has its own. The prime is the base lending rate at a commercial bank, the rate it charges its biggest and best clients.

- The general meaning of low unemployment figures is that the economy is healthy and there are plenty of jobs, but when the unemployment rate gets too low, it could indicate that wages will rise in an inflationary manner, and the Fed will stomp on the brakes. Then, up go interest rates. When unemployment falls below 3 to 4 percent, concern rises.

- The Gross National Product also offers clues. A gently rising GNP usually means a healthy economy, but grossly elevated figures also hint at inflation. A slowdown in the rate of growth in the GNP sends the opposite message; rates, eventually, will come down. GNP growth of 3 percent to 5 percent a year makes most U.S. presidents happy.

- Gold and the inflation rate tend to move in the same direction. And, as we've learned, inflation leads to higher interest rates. When people start selling gold, the price falls, indicating that investors are not expecting high inflation, and therefore interest rates will decline.

- In recent years, however, gold has sometimes failed to react in a predictable manner to economic events, partly because the supply of gold itself has been increasing fairly quickly.

- The Dow Jones Utility Average long has been regarded as a proxy for interest rates; utilities, which have had to borrow massive amounts of money to finance construction and other capital needs, have been particularly sensitive to interest rates.

If the stocks of light and power companies are rising, investors expect higher profits, and therefore may foresee lower interest rates. Conversely, when stock prices decline, less profitability is expected, perhaps because higher rates are anticipated.

Some experts say that the performance of gas and electric companies is not tied as closely to interest rates as it once was, so fluctuations don't have the impact on their earnings that they used to. However, as long as investors still believe otherwise, the utility index remains a barometer of interest rate expectations.

The Dow utility index can be found charted daily in the *Wall Street Journal* and in the business sections of many other papers.

Oddly enough, history shows that high interest rates alone have not been sufficient to lure people into greater savings levels. But they have been enough to tempt savers to move from the stock market or real estate into interest-bearing accounts, especially those that proffer exceptional safety, such as government issues.

RESPONDING TO RATES

Savers' recommended strategies vary with the particular interest rate scenarios:

- equilibrium
- ascending rates
- descending rates

STABILITY

Rates that stay relatively stable, moving neither up nor down by a significant number of percentage points over a prolonged period of time, create a climate in which financial institutions compete the most aggressively to attract investors. Since the deregulation of financial institutions, the savings institutions have added weapons to their arsenal for the skirmishes. This is the time to be a super shopper.

THE RISING TIDE

When the economy is bubbling and the Fed nudges short-term rates up to keep inflation down, it is the best of times for savers. There is a lot of incentive for staying in very secure, cash-equivalent investments. They offer safety, plus about the best yields around.

The saver should put money in short-term certificates of deposit (to be cashed in and reinvested as rates edge up) or in a money market fund. An unexciting plan, perhaps, but it's hard to get hurt by such conservatism.

When interest rates do begin mounting rapidly, stay in the shortest-term accounts, or in a money market fund that has proven very responsive to rate changes. This is a time for waiting, observing the market, and being poised to lock in top rates in the future.

INFLATION PLUS HIGH RATES

If inflation accompanies the rising rates, put a larger percentage of your funds into real estate, or perhaps use some of the new insured accounts that are indexed to gold or other commodities. As long as the principal amount of the account is insured, the risk on the earnings may be acceptable. The best of these accounts offer a guaranteed minimum interest rate, and an even better rate if gold, a commodities index, or some other specific indicator rises.

SLACKING OFF

In the face of sure signs of an economic slowdown, a saver should make the shift to long-term government bonds. Not only does this lock in favorable rates, but it also offers profits should it become necessary to cash in the bonds. Bond prices will soar as interest rates head down, making them a particularly attractive option.

Keep an eye on the Treasury Bond rate. When the T-Bond falls half a point or more, that's a reliable signal to move into longer-term CDs or other long-term instruments. When bond rates dip, banks typically take several months before dropping CD rates, so there are several weeks during which savers can lock in high rates before they vanish.

CLOSE IS GOOD ENOUGH

Don't panic if you miss the market peak or are late in anticipating a reversal. Almost no one times the market perfectly.

Since it is difficult to tell when rates have peaked, savers may want to shift funds gradually from short-term to longer-term maturities when a summit seems near. If perhaps 10 percent of funds is moved from short to longer maturities one month at a time, it will be easier for savers to hit the peak and lock up some of the most significant rates.

Many investor newsletters offer information on how to find the best interest rates around—either the lowest rates on credit cards, mortgages, and other loans, or the highest rates on money markets, certificates of deposit, or other accounts. These publications are available through subscription, but many can be found in the public library, or as part of computerized financial databases.

"Bank Credit Card Observer"—3806 Old Lincoln Highway, Kendall Park, NJ 08824. This organization offers a list of ten lowest rate issuers nationwide, as well as other interest-related information.
"NROCA Newsletter"—NROCA Press, Box 12066, Dallas, Texas 75225. NROCA provides an array of information on currently available rates.
"RAM Bancard Update"—Box 1700 (Colleges Estates), Frederick, MD 21701. This newsletter has a list of

no-fee and low-interest credit card issuers; and offers other data.

Rategram, The Bradshaw Financial Group, 253 Channing Way, Suite 13, San Rafael, CA 94903. This biweekly interest rate service also is available on computer, through The Source.

FIGURING EARNINGS

Understanding the behavior of interest rates, however, is only half of the problem. Figuring the costs and returns on interest-bearing accounts is the other half. While this may seem technically difficult at first glance, there are quick and accurate methods for computing in advance, the interest paid and interest earned. Those techniques will be reviewed in the chapter ahead.

CHAPTER 9

Finding the Best Rates; Figuring Earnings

*"Genius is nothing but a greater aptitude
for patience."*

GEORGE LOUIS LECLERC DE BUFFON

"**P**erhaps you think the difference between a full-sized car and a compact is about $10,000. Actually the difference is more like a million dollars," Paul Richard of the National Center for Financial Education once wrote. "Consider this. Borrowing $25,000 for a new car over four years will cost about $634 a month while borrowing just $15,000 will cost only $381 a month. At age 30 begin saving the difference, $253 a month, for 35 years.

"Earning an 8 percent average rate of return, it will swell to $580,352. If one were to get monthly payments of $4,479 from that sum from ages 65 to 90 (some predictions are that there will be over 250 thousand people over the age of 100 in America in the 21st century) the total amount collected would be $1.3 million.

"It's the magic of compound interest," Richard said. "But it isn't retroactive. One must save now to enjoy the benefits of compound interest in the future."

We've all been dazzled at one time or another by the startling cost of credit. Conversely, we've seen the amazing things that compounding interest rates, the addition of just one-half of one percent in interest or just another year of accumulation, may do to your savings total.

DO IT YOURSELF

While the examples may provide a motivation to save and an incentive to understand interest rates, at some point you need to know how to apply this kind of information to your own situation. It is most important that savers find ways to calculate their own rates of return, not only to compare different kinds of savings products, but also to check for themselves that sales claims are accurate. Savers can also look into the future and plan ahead, when they have the mathematical tools.

This chapter does not, however, set out to teach readers how to compute each and every interest rate scenario that can arise. Rather, some concepts will be introduced, and guidelines as to where to find the information will be given. There are many places to turn for help. The calculations can be done easily and simply, even by those without a technical background or a talent for math.

RULE OF 72

For starters, one simple computation gives the saver an uncomplicated way to think about a rate under consideration. It is called the Rule of 72, and it is a formula for approximating the time required for any amount of money to double at a given compound interest rate.

Simply divide 72 by the interest rate, and that number will be the years required to multiply the money two-fold. For example, it will take six years for, say, $100 to double at a compound annual rate of 12 percent: 72 divided by 12

116

Table 9–1
The Rule of 72 at Work

5% interest into 72	=	Slightly more than 14 yrs. and 4 mos. to double
8% interest into 72	=	9 yrs. to double
10% interest into 72	=	Slightly more than 7 yrs. and 2 mos. to double

---

equals 6. Even at lower rates, the wizardry of compounding is impressive.

FIGURING AHEAD

While the Rule of 72 tells something specific about what a dollar will be worth at some distant time, there are many other money problems that also require determining future values.

The 13 situations that follow are examples of everyday math problems that can be solved by knowing how to figure the future value of money. Answers are at the end of the chapter.

FUTURE VALUE OF A DOLLAR

A. If you have $1,500 to invest today in an account that pays an 8 percent interest rate compounded annually, what will the investment be worth in 20 years?

B. What rate of interest must you earn on a $2,500 investment for it to be worth $3,500 in 3 years, assuming the interest is compounded monthly?

C. How do these returns compare—If you were offered a 10 percent return compounded monthly for 4 years, and a 10.5 return compounded annually for 4 years, which is the better deal?

117

FUTURE VALUE PER PERIOD

The future value per period is the basic compound interest function for a series of repeated deposits. This calculation can be used in the following two situations:

D. How much more would your Individual Retirement Account be worth if you made regular deposits of $150 to the account at the beginning of each month rather than at the end? Assume that payments will be made for 3 years, and the account earns 10 percent compounded monthly.

E. How long will it take to save $25,000 if you deposit $250 each quarter into an account that pays 12 percent, compounded quarterly?

A SINKING FUND

If you want to make a series of equal deposits for a determined future obligation or goal, the deposit amount will be computed on the basis of a sinking fund. While your deposit fund increases, the amount still to be saved to reach the goal or obligation sinks. You can use a sinking-fund method to figure problems **F** and **G**:

F. How large a savings deposit will you need to make each month to pay your son's college tuition? He starts college in 10 years; his tuition will be $20,000, and you've found an account that guarantees a 10 percent yield, compounded monthly.

G. If you are able to save only $50 per month, how long would it take—at a 7 percent interest yield compounded monthly—to save enough to add a $10,000 room onto your house?

PRESENT VALUE

To determine how much you must put in an account today to achieve a certain sum at some future date, you must determine the present value of $1. Calculating the present value involves a single advance payment or deposit, unlike the sinking fund, which requires a series of deposits. The present-value function will help you answer such questions as the next two:

H. How much should be paid for a zero-coupon bond that earns a 10 percent rate of interest and that will be worth $30,000 in 15 years? Zero coupon bonds, generally, earn interest semiannually.

I. You have $50,000, but you know that in 5 years you will need $75,000. What rate of interest, compounded monthly, must you earn in order to meet that goal?

PRESENT VALUE PER PERIOD

Like its future value, the present value of a dollar also can be computed over a period of time. The present-value-per-period technique is useful in finding solutions in the following situations:

J. How much would a 12 percent annuity (compounded monthly) be worth today if the insurance company were paying you $300 each month for the next 5 years?

K. What would the annuity above be worth at present if payments of $1,800 were being made only semiannually?

AMORTIZATION

Because it is used to answer questions about time payments, partial payment to amortize $1 is a concept to which many consumers have already been introduced. It is used to determine a succession of repeated payments or withdrawals, and can solve the following types of problems:

L. If your $200,000 retirement 401(k) rolls over when you retire, and you put the money into an account paying 9 percent compounded monthly, what is the maximum amount you can withdraw from that account each month and still have the money last 15 years?

119

M. The 30-year mortgage on your new home will be for $250,000 at 12.5 percent interest compounded monthly. What is your monthly payment? How much principal will you still owe after making payments for 20 years?

THE EASY WAY OUT

Though these may be everyday questions, it would seem to take years of know-how to do the arithmetic. Not really. Someone else has figured ways to make it much simpler. The work has been done for you.

Perhaps the easiest solution to the problem of computing costs and earnings is to drive to practically any general-interest bookstore and buy a volume of compound interest tables. These manuals, which offer step-by-step instructions to answering the questions in this chapter and many more, can be found in the business book section.

A BOOK ON THE TABLES

Barron's Financial Tables for Better Money Management is one such primer that the saver may find helpful. Other sources can be found in the suggested reading list on page 235. For those who want more practical self-help tools, some handbooks present not only the tables but also the mathematical formulas used in factoring the calculations.

ELECTRONIC WONDERS

Several reasonably priced, hand-held calculators can simply and easily produce these figures as well. The Texas Instruments Business Analyst II business calculator for example computes interest and balances, interest rate conversions, compound interest calculations, annuity calculations, home mortgage payments, remaining balances for a home mortgage, and other operations helpful to savers. And don't worry, it isn't necessary to be a math genius to use the calculator. It comes with a handbook.

PROGRAMMERS TO THE RESCUE

In addition, a variety of desk-top computer programs offer these applications. Some software packages for personal portfolio management include comprehensive compound interest tables. For a saver who uses these functions regularly and already has a computer, the programs can be handy and quick. However, it would be quite costly to buy a home computer and the necessary software solely for this purpose.

WHAT WILL THE MARKET PAY?

Before you figure your earnings, though, you need to know what sort of an interest rate is reasonable, given the current climate and for the near and long-term outlook. Earlier chapters offered bellwethers for anticipating market direction; the sources suggested in the following pages can help in determining how well or how pitifully you may be able to do at any given point.

MONEY RATES

When browsing for a savings instrument and comparing rates, it helps to know the standard going rate for similar products. Finding current rates requires nothing more than perusing the business section of a daily newspaper or picking up a copy of the *Wall Street Journal*.

CHECK THE FINE PRINT

In the agate pages of the newspaper (those toward the back set in tiny print) under a section usually headed "money rates," key U.S. and foreign annual interest rates are listed. The chart will include the prime rate, the base rate on corporate loans charged by the large, or money center, commercial banks. It will list the federal funds rate; the discount rate charged by the Federal Reserve Bank of New York; certificate of deposit rates for various maturities; Treasury Bill yields; Federal Home Loan Mortgage Corporation yields on the most recent 30-year mortgage commitments; and posted yields on Federal National Mortgage Association, or Fannie Mae, 30-year instruments. The 30-day rate of return on the Merrill Lynch Ready Asset Trust may also be included as a reference point.

Other rates posted on these charts may not be as relevant to savers, but they are of some use when scouting trends. They include the rate for call money, or the charge on loans to brokers on stock exchange collateral; commercial paper, which is short-term corporate obligations; bankers' acceptances, negotiable, bank-backed business credit instruments used in foreign trade; the London Interbank Offered Rates (Libor), which is used by currency traders; and several other items.

Some local newspapers print a rate chart on local and regional financial institutions, but probably not all banks, savings and loans, or thrift and loans will be represented.

Most weekly and monthly business publications (*Business Week* and *Money* are two) also carry the rates, but the numbers sometimes aren't as fresh as newspaper rates. There is a greater lag time for magazines between the collection of information and its printing and distribution.

GUIDELINE RATES

Of necessity, the publicly reported rates often depict either average rates or the most representative rate available. Each bank, for example, sets its own prime rate, so the exact prime for each financial institution, even each major bank, would be impossible to list. The prime rate listed in the newspaper is only an average indicator.

WATCH THE NEWSPAPER ADS

To find the most current rate for a specific financial institution, go on back to local and national newspapers. Since newspaper advertisements can be placed easily and with short lead time, most financial institutions use this outlet for announcing changes in rates, terms, and details for their products. News stories and newspaper ads are the front line on information.

Frequently, the institutions offering the most competitive rates are doing the most advertising. For one reason or another, they've decided to attract more funds (they may be planning to provide funding for a major construction project or corporate deal), and the best way to do that is to beat out the competition with the introduction of higher rates on appropriate accounts.

In addition, a number of national newsletters track rates on a weekly, monthly, or quarterly basis and can help savers pinpoint the most competitive interests nationwide. Subscriptions are available at varying prices, and many libraries carry these newsletters in the business information section.

When searching out rates, the saver will find many advertisers offering tax-sheltered, tax-free, double tax-free, or other tax-advantaged accounts. Some people will want and need these savings vehicles; others may not. But don't rule out tax-favored accounts until you've read about the tax implications of your savings in the chapter ahead.

Solutions to problems on pages 117-19: Each of these answers has been derived by consulting comprehensive compound interest rate tables.

  A. $6,991.50.

  B. 11.25 percent.

  C. 10 percent compounded monthly provides the higher return.

  D. If deposited at the end of the month, the amount would be $6,267.27. Deposited at the beginning, it would total $6,319.50. The difference? $52.23.

E. 47 quarters, or just over 11 years and 8 months.

F. Your payments will be $97.64 per month.

G. It would take just under 7 years to save the $10,000.

H. The zero-coupon bond should cost $6,941.31.

I. Your goal will be achieved in an account yielding around 8 percent.

J. The present value of the annuity would be $13,846.51.

K. The present value now would be $13,153.23.

L. You can make monthly payments to yourself of $2,149.20 for the next 15 years, and the money will hold out.

M. The monthly payments will be $2,668.25. After making those payments for 20 years, you will still owe $182,282.42 on your home.

CHAPTER 10

The Tax Implications
of Savings

"There is one difference between a tax collector and a taxidermist—the taxidermist leaves the hide."

MORTIMER CAPLAN, FORMER DIRECTOR
OF THE INTERNAL REVENUE SERVICE

Albert Einstein once said that the hardest thing in the world to understand was income taxes, and Einstein was long gone by the time the Tax Reform Act of 1986 and its correctional piece, the Technical and Miscellaneous Revenue Act of 1988, were passed by Congress. Imagine how Einstein would feel now.

TAX TRAUMA

The first piece of legislation—originally ballyhooed as tax-simplification—fills a book ten inches thick that weighs more than 33 pounds. TRA incorporated changes in more than 2.7 million subsections of the tax code.

While it is true that the 1986 law dramatically cut taxes for some Americans and eliminated them altogether for a handful, it did not abolish a disturbing fact of life for the majority of us: The most intimidating single financial obli-

125

gation most Americans face each year is taxes. And the more money you earn, the worse it is. It was estimated that in 1989, Americans paid $146.6 billion in federal taxes alone.

WORKING FOR THE GOVERNMENT

The 1986 law created two primary federal tax brackets, 15 and 28 percent, with a 33 percent tax applicable to a portion of the incomes of high-earners.

"It will take more than one-third of the year and two hours and forty-five minutes of each eight hours' earnings by the average middle-income taxpayer to produce one person's share of the 1988 tax bill," wrote Jeff A. Schnepper in his 1989 edition of *How to Pay Zero Taxes.*

TAXES SAP SAVINGS

Economist Martin Feldstein, in a 1988 *Wall Street Journal* opinion piece, pointed out that taxes still present a critical problem to savers.

"A major reason we Americans save so little is that taxes still take most of the real return on additional savings," Feldstein wrote. "Consider a taxpayer who earns a 9 percent nominal return on a bond and expects inflation to average

Figure 10-1   **Tax Freedom Day**

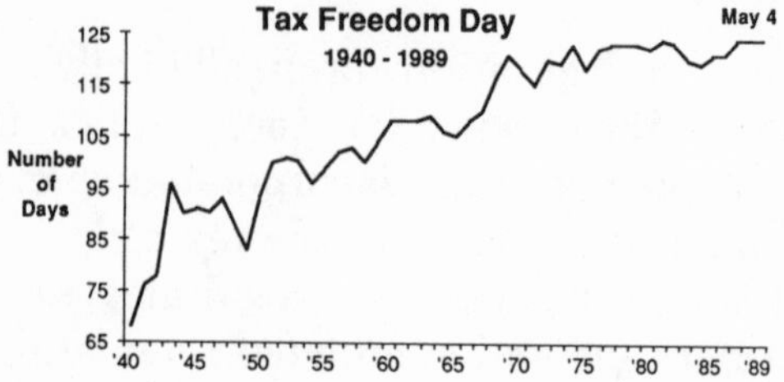

Source: Tax Foundation news release

Figure 10–2   **1989 Tax Bite in 8-Hour Day**

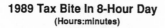

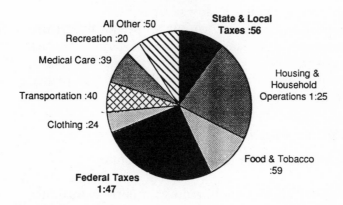

1989 Tax Bite In 8-Hour Day
(Hours:minutes)

All Other :50
Recreation :20
Medical Care :39
Transportation :40
Clothing :24
Federal Taxes 1:47
State & Local Taxes :56
Housing & Household Operations 1:25
Food & Tobacco :59

Source: Tax Foundation news release

5 percent a year during the life of the bond. His expected pretax real return is thus 4 percent. If the taxpayer has a 28 percent marginal federal income-tax rate and an effective 5 percent state income-tax rate, he faces a combined marginal tax rate that takes one-third of his nominal 9 percent return. His after-tax nominal rate of return is therefore only 6 percent. With a 5 percent expected inflation, the real after-tax return is only 1 percent.

"Thus taxes reduce the real return to 1 percent from 4 percent because the tax law does not correctly distinguish between real interest income and the payments that just offset the inflationary erosion of the value of the debt. Even with a 33 percent combined federal and state statutory tax rate, the effective tax on real interest income is 75 percent."

Feldstein was building a case for federal tax law reform that provides a greater incentive to save. In doing so, he made one thing clear, that the smart and effective investor pays close attention to taxes.

Even without his lucid arguments, most savers realize that any expense that chews up 15 to 33 percent of income must be taken seriously. An attack on tax bites may be the most productive battle any saver fights.

This chapter doesn't set out to provide everything there is to know about taxes. There are 600-page books that must be rewritten every year that try to do that. But some guiding principles are offered, along with some tips to help cope with tax afflictions.

COMBAT PLAN

The battle must be waged on two fronts:

- Reducing the tax bite on your current income
- Choosing savings accounts and withdrawing funds from them carefully, so as not to create unnecessary tax obligations

Some of the same concepts apply to both of these campaigns. For one thing, in both, it's crucial to grasp the difference between a *tax deduction* and a *tax credit*.

TAX DEDUCTION

A tax deduction, or excludable income, lowers income subject to taxes, and therefore your tax obligation. If you are in the 28 percent bracket, for example, each dollar converted to excludable income can be equated to getting a 28 percent after-tax raise. For this reason, 401(k)s, Keoghs, and nontaxable remuneration for services (such as health benefit plans, group term life insurance, and certain employer educational assistance) are valuable tax tools.

Some income, such as that from most municipal bonds, is exempt from federal taxes altogether. The higher your tax bracket, the more worthwhile they become.

TAX CREDIT

But even more rewarding than tax deductions and excludable income are tax credits. A credit is a dollar-for-dollar reduction in your tax liability. If the credit is for $100, then $100 is lopped off your tax bill. It is the best kind of tax benefit to have.

Typical tax credits include the earned income credit, credit for excess Social Security tax paid, and the child and dependent care credit. Elderly and disabled persons, such as the blind, may be eligible for tax credits as well.

INCOME IDENTIFICATION

An easy way to approach tax problems is by understanding four basic types of income:

- Taxable
- Tax-free
- Tax-deferred
- Tax-sheltered

What follows is a review of some of the types of income in each of the four categories. Readers of this book should bear in mind that since the tax law continually changes, tax advantages that exist today may not be available tomorrow.

TAXABLE INCOME

Taxable income includes currently paid salaries, commissions, royalties, bonuses, ordinary business profits, interest on savings accounts, bonds, and so forth.

Most of the money we *earn* is subject to taxes. Gross income can be reduced by certain deductions, and it is on that lower amount that taxes are computed.

While a person may reduce his or her tax obligation, the Alternative Minimum Tax, a law enacted to close certain tax loopholes (see glossary), virtually ensures that any citizen with significant income will pay something each year to the IRS.

TAX-FREE INCOME

Municipal bonds are the tax-free vehicle with which most savers are likely to be familiar. But there are other forms of income that are not taxable, aside from tax-free bonds. They include certain prizes, such as the Pulitzer or Nobel Peace prizes. On a more mundane level, if you receive a scholarship for school tuition or find yourself the beneficiary of a life insurance policy, those too generally will be tax-free.

DEFERRED TAXES

A great deal of space has been devoted to tax-deferred income in earlier chapters. This type of income is earned now, but tax payments are put off until a later date. Earnings on a qualified retirement program, IRAs and funds held in life insurance policies and annuities fall into this category. The income from U.S. savings bonds is also tax-deferred until the bonds are cashed in.

There are two motives for deferring taxes whenever possible:

- Inflation
- The time value of money

INFLATION ON YOUR SIDE

Inflation, as mentioned earlier, can devastate savings, but deferring taxes helps mitigate the impact. Not only do you continue to receive earnings on the money you've postponed handing over to the government, but also when you finally do pay the tax, you pay it in dollars that are worth less.

If you have a $1 tax obligation today that is based on the 33 percent tax bracket, you lose 33 percent of your purchasing or earning power if you pay the tax. But if you postpone the tax and pay it, say 12 years from now, and inflation during that time averages 6 percent per year, you would still be paying the $1, but you would be paying it with one-half of the purchasing power you would have had if paid today (assuming, of course, that tax rates don't change in the meantime).

MARKING TIME

The time value of money means also that investing money before it is shrunken by taxes allows faster compounding.

Example: If you had $100 and were in the top tax bracket, you may pay $33 in taxes on that money. There would be $67 left out of the $100 to invest. If held for 10 years in an account paying 7 percent compounded annually, your money would grow to $110.42.

But if you had the full $100 and put it in that same account paying 7 percent compounded annual interest, after 10 years your savings and interest would amount to $196.72. You would have to pay taxes on the initial $100 plus taxes

---

Figure 10–3   **Comparison of Taxable and Tax-Deferred Accumulation**

	10 years	20 years	30 years
■ Tax-deferred IRA	$35,062	$126,005	$361,886
☐ Taxable account	$29,903	$89,837	$209,959
$ you are ahead with tax deferral	$5,159	$36,168	$151,927
% you are ahead with tax deferral	17%	40%	72%

Source: The Source: A Guiide for Financial Planners

---

on the earnings, for a total tax obligation of $64.92. Your $100 would now be worth $131.80 after taxes, $21.38 more than in the preceding case. Your earnings have tripled.

And if you had retired by that time, you may be in a lower tax bracket, making your savings even greater.

IRS PAID UP FRONT

If you have any doubt about the time value of money, just consider the IRS's own policy. The tax man requires withholding of taxes, or estimation and prepayment of taxes, but pays no interest on funds over-withheld.

One sure-fire way to maximize the time value of your money is to withhold as little, or pay as little withholding or estimated tax, as possible (without under-withholding and risking penalties) and therefore have the use and availability of these tax funds for as long as legally feasible.

SHELTERING INCOME

The fourth category, sheltered income, is used by investors to legally avoid or reduce tax liabilities. Several tax techniques, including depreciation and pass-through income, are employed for sheltering purposes.

A number of savings and investment devices fall into this category. However, the term "tax shelter" fell into disfavor in the 1980s when a proliferation of obviously abusive tax shelter schemes arose, such as one to market lithographic rights to a design and another involving buying Bibles in bulk for charitable distribution at a marked-up price.

SAVER BEWARE

Except for real estate, municipal bonds, and retirement savings plans, economist Paul Erdman warns Americans away from most tax shelters, except municipal bonds and other clearly understandable vehicles. "I would avoid being talked into investing in any other type of fancy tax shelters, be they oil and gas ventures, R&D schemes or race horses. Too often you end up 'saving' taxes but also losing all your money," he wrote in one of his books. Who needs such grief, he asked.

While the Tax Reform Act of 1986 took the wind out of the sails of many tax shelters, it did not eliminate them altogether. The reformed tax law said, essentially, tax-shelter losses are deductible only against other tax-shelter income, or at the termination of the activity. Otherwise such a loss would be disqualified.

While it is true that many legitimate and profitable tax shelters exist, most of them are not suitable for savers because they almost invariably involve high-risk ventures.

TAX MANAGEMENT OF SAVINGS

Several types of tax-favored investments are suitable for conservative-thinking savers, however. Earlier chapters covered the tax advantages of home ownership and voluntary, qualified pension plans. In the next section of the book, each of the vehicles will be explained in additional detail. Briefly, they include:

- Annuities and other life insurance products
- Treasury securities (exempt from state taxes)
- Municipal bonds (triple-exempt in certain regions)

AN UNBIASED APPRAISAL

While awareness of tax implications is important for savers, you should not let tax advantages blind you to the basic strength and weakness of a savings instrument. Before buying a product that promises a tax savings, compare it with taxable alternatives.

There is a standard method for making that comparison. All that is necessary is to divide the tax exempt yield by 1 minus your tax bracket, expressed as a decimal. If you are in the 28 percent federal tax bracket and you are contemplating the purchase of a municipal bond yielding 7 percent, the calculation would look like this:

7 percent divided 0.72 (1–1.28) = 9.72.

To beat out the municipal bond, a taxable investment would have to yield 9.72 percent.

If after this calculation, the taxable yield and the tax-exempt yield turn out to be the same, many experts suggest opting for the tax-exempt alternative. They figure that after TRA 1986, taxes became as low as they ever would be. Pressure on the government to improve the budget deficit likely would continue, probably driving taxes higher.

TAXES NEVER RETIRE

For most of your adult life you've probably heard tax experts and financial advisers talk of the beauty of "deferring taxes until retirement," at which time you supposedly will be in a lower tax bracket. Well, you may indeed be in a lower tax bracket than that of your prime income-producing years, but that doesn't mean your tax responsibilities, and perhaps some very big tax decisions, are past.

The plethora of ads for IRAs and other retirement savings products talk mainly about putting money into retirement plans. Few mention the tax perils of withdrawing the funds.

"But what happens when you're ready to tap into your retirement cache?" asked *Personal Investor* magazine in a 1989 article. "Information about withdrawing money from IRAs, Keoghs, 401(k)s or similar plans isn't so readily available."

Did you know, for instance, that . . .

- the Internal Revenue Service slaps on a 10 percent penalty on withdrawals made from most qualified retirement plans and IRAs before age 59½? This penalty is added to the tax otherwise due on withdrawal.

- if you fail to withdraw the required minimum amount from your IRA after you reach age 70½, the IRS will hit you with a 50 percent excise tax on the amount by which you fall short?
- there is a 15 percent excise for taking too much from IRAs and other retirement plans in one year? The so-called success tax applies to individuals who receive large amounts of money in either annual distributions or a lump sum. In 1989, the tax applied to annual distributions of more than $150,000 or lump-sum distributions of more than $750,000, and those figures are indexed for inflation each year.
- certain, but not all, retirement arrangements allow five-year income averaging for lump-sum withdrawals? The tax liability can be spread out over five years on 401(k)s, Keoghs, and other qualified plans, but not on IRAs and SEPs.

These are only a few of the withdrawal conditions that a retiree should know about—before accepting the gold watch, not after.

WISE WITHDRAWALS

The tax twists go on and on. All of them cannot be listed and explained here.

But the message is thunderously loud and lightning-clear. Not only is professional help constructive when planning for taxes; it is priceless when planning for retirement. Fortunately many corporations, labor unions, and senior citizens organizations offer free retirement counseling. Also, retirement planning, more and more, is being offered by specialists in the field, for a fee. And retirement planning classes often are available through community colleges and adult school programs.

CRASH COURSE ON COLLEGE

Ideally, families should begin preparing to meet college costs from the day the prospective student is born, since paying for a child's college education is probably the most intensive cash drain a family faces. Even so, a 1984 Roper Poll indicated that fewer than half of parents who expected their children to attend college set aside money in advance for that purpose.

When planning ahead, a family should figure on tuition and associated fees increasing by an annual rate of 6 percent to 10 percent. Table 10-1 reflects *Newsday* newspaper estimates of rate increases by the year 2005, and the subsequent savings required to meet costs for children born in 1986. The amount of savings required is based on equal deposits over 17 years.

SHELTER OR TRANSFER

Because saving for college is a long-term proposition, probably the best types of accounts to use for this purpose have a tax advantage of some kind. They either transfer parents' income to children and defer taxes until the youngsters can pay the tax at their own rate, or, at the very least, allow the tax-free compounding of earnings until the students must pay school expenses.

Table 10-1
Saving For College in 2005

College/University	Total Tuition 1987	Total Tuition 2005	Estimated Savings Required by 2005 Annual	Estimated Savings Required by 2005 Monthly
Public 2-Yr.	$ 1,415	$ 4,040	$ 118	$ 10
Public 4-Yr.	5,945	16,969	499	42
Private 4-Yr.	31,105	88,778	2,611	220
Selective Private	49,259	140,600	4,135	345

Even a tax-free instrument may do the job, such as a tax-free zero-coupon municipal bond. More information on these instruments is offered in Chapter 14, which covers government securities.

BANKING ON BONDS

A new way to save for college is through U.S. Series EE savings bonds. As of 1990, the Series EE bond interest escapes taxation as long as the bonds are used to pay for such education costs as tuition.

This special tax treatment, however, is subject to several conditions:

- The bonds must be kept in a parent's name rather than the child's. Parents must be 24 years or older.
- The bonds must be purchased by the parents. Those bought by grandparents, godparents, or others do not qualify.

Figure 10–4 **EE Bonds for College Saving**

The earlier you start saving, the more you will have when your child is ready for college. For example:

Child's Age Now*	Value† at Age 18 Based on Monthly Allotments of:	
	$50.00	$100.00
1	$17,356.08	$34,712.16
6	10,328.96	20,657.92
10	6,025.72	12,051.44
12	4,226.88	8,453.76

*Current tax law requires children age 5 and above to have a Social Security number.

†Assumes annual interest rate of 6 percent (current minimum rate) and 10-year interest extension. Rate could be higher.
Source: US Government

- The tax-free provision is phased out when modified adjusted gross income is in the $60,000 to $90,000 range on joint returns or $40,000 to $55,000 for those filing singly. These amounts are indexed beginning in 1990.
- Bonds issued before December 31, 1989, cannot be converted to the program.

More details about savings bonds can be found in the section on government securities, Chapter 14.

CUSTODIAL ACCOUNTS

Because they require the actual transfer of assets to the minor, the Uniform Gift to Minors Act (UGMA) and the Uniform Transfers to Minors Act (UTMA, available in 30 states) aren't savings vehicles for the parent. Once the assets are transferred to a child, parents lose control. However, these accounts can provide income or assets to pay for college.

UGMA accounts allow you to include only money (bank, savings and loan, credit union, and money market accounts), securities, annuities, and in some states, insurance policies.

The UTMA, on the other hand, lets you transfer any kind of property, including real estate, paintings, or even limited partnership interests, to your child.

Contributions to these accounts qualify for the $10,000 annual exclusion from the gift tax. The limit is $20,000 annually if a spouse joins in the gift-giving. Both accounts require you to name a custodian who controls the assets until the child reaches adulthood, age 18 in many states, but a parent can be the custodian.

UTMAs and UGMAs can be easily set up with forms obtained from a broker or bank. No legal fees are involved. However, a careful study of how much money can be transferred to a dependent in this way should be made. Children under age 14 must pay taxes at their parents' rate for any unearned income over $1,000. Most earnings below that amount would be taxed at a lower amount.

TUITION TRUST

High-income parents who want to permanently give certain assets to offspring, for college or any other purpose, should consider establishing a trust. A sizable chunk of income is taxable to the trust itself, rather than the child, and therefore avoids being taxed at the parents' higher rate. Legal help in setting up a trust is necessary, and tax returns must be filed separately each year for the trust.

HINDRANCE

With a UTMA, UGMA, or a trust, an important feature to keep in mind is that the assets belong to the child and will be considered as such if he or she applies for financial aid once the child reaches college. Under a commonly used formula for determining student eligibility for aid, students are expected to contribute 35 percent of their available assets each year to college costs. A parent's subsidy is expected to be a much lower percent of assets.

Where to Find Expert Tax Help

Except for taxpayers in the lowest bracket who may not want to bother to itemize their deductions, it is more important than ever to get professional help in tax preparation.

Ideally, assistance should be sought from either a certified public accountant or an enrolled agent. Tax attorneys can do the job, but usually they do not actually prepare tax statements; rather, they represent clients in court.

A CPA will prepare returns, represent taxpayers before the IRS, and do tax planning. For tax planning, the process of adapting financial activities so as to best take advantage of the tax code in the years ahead, a CPA or a tax lawyer can be most effective.

An enrolled agent is a tax professional licensed by the federal government to represent taxpayers before the Internal Revenue Service. No license is required to prepare the returns themselves.

In case of an audit, it is comforting to have the highest level of professional assistance and emotional support possible.

Even for those who will use a professional tax adviser, some personal background in the current tax code is extremely instructional when budgeting and finding places to maximize the growth of savings.

There are many excellent books on the market. It is essential, however, to find the most up-to-date book available, preferably one published in the year in which you will be using it. Because tax codes change somewhat almost every year, outdated information is more than detrimental; it is dangerous. The *World Almanac* prints the major provisions of the latest tax code each year, but other books offer better interpretations.

To get help from the IRS itself you may call one of two national hotlines, 1-800-424-1040 to speak to a representative or 1-800-424-3676 to order IRS publications or tax forms.

PART
4

Financial Institutions and Savings Products

CHAPTER 11

Where to Save

*"Forget about a return on my investment.
I want a return of my investment."*

WILL ROGERS

As surely as the swallows return to San Juan Capistrano in the spring, business journalists joyfully announce the previous year's best performing investments each January.

APPRECIATING ART

And the 1988 winners according to *Money* magazine were—oats on the futures market, California real estate, fine art, vintage powerboats, and gems. Contemporary art had a good year, with a silkscreen by Harry Shokler appreciating 185 percent and paintings by the Cleveland School, a group of social realists from the 1920s and 1930s, doubling in value. A generous gainer was tsavorite, a rare variety of garnet found primarily in East Africa, up 20 percent in one year. One 16.6-carat specimen of the grass-green stone soared in value to $125,000.

If your intuition had been finely tuned and you had the instincts of a pack rat, you might have realized the importance of hanging on to translucent acrylic handbags from the 1950s (up 50 percent) or a first edition of Stephen King's classic *The Dark Tower: The Gunslinger* ($20 when published in 1982, $525 in 1989).

Pretty impressive, if you had either superior good taste or dumb luck. You probably wish dearly for dumb luck. So does everyone else.

LUCK ISN'T ENOUGH

No question about it, collectibles are a lot more fun than cold cash. Nevertheless, a lot more people have made money with judiciously planned savings, through making wise purchases of cars and real estate, and by anticipating interest rate changes and investigating accordingly, than ever made a fortune on a bundle of comic books.

While the highest yield available is certainly a key consideration in making savings choices, return on investment is not the single most important factor in deciding how to invest savings.

THE SLY STANDARD

Bankers quip that smart savers follow the "SLY" principle. SLY stands for:

- Safety
- Liquidity
- Yield

SCARED INTO SECLUSION

Safety has become a major worry since two news-grabbing episodes of the '80s.

The stock market crash of October 19, 1987, sent many investors fleeing from the equities market into more secure havens for their funds. Even as long after the crash as January 1989, institutional investors were keeping higher cash positions than they'd held since mid-year 1984.

Then as 1988 rolled to a close, the insurance crisis in the savings and loan industry had reached volcanic proportions as well. A record number of troubled institutions were being closed, and government officials, not too discreetly, began to talk of the possibility of suspending government insurance for savings and loans. Savers, who had been gobbling up unsustainable high rates at troubled institutions, suddenly had a lot of questions. If the government reneges on one kind of federal insurance, is any insurance safe?

A REALISTIC STANDARD OF SAFETY

There is no completely risk-free place to keep money. *Dessauer's Journal of Financial Markets* reported the story of a New England man who became so frightened over bank safety that he withdrew his account and put stacks of bills into his safety deposit box:

"What he forgot was a recent story of how a few policemen cooperated with criminals to rob the safe deposit vault in another Massachusetts bank. There is little or no insurance on the contents of a safe deposit box, so in a robbery the gentleman's cash would be gone. He had not found a 'safe haven' for his cash; he exchanged one risk for another," claimed Dessauer.

HAVE A LITTLE FAITH

Dessauer had a point, but no depositors thus far have lost their federally insured deposits, and robberies of deposit boxes are extremely rare.

The sad part of Dessauer's story is that the silly man abandoned one remarkably safe account for an equally safe place, but one that offered no possibility of growth in value. In fact, inflation would eat away at the worth of his cash, draining away much of its value. At some point we have to accept a certain level of risk. It is our main job to minimize that risk as much as reasonably possible.

However slight the consolation, the panic-stricken man in Dessauer's little story had, at least, preserved the liquidity of his account.

TAKE THE MONEY AND RUN

Liquidity always is important when dealing with assets. Even the rarest automobile in the world is worthless, from an investor's point of view, if nobody is willing to buy the dust-collecting antiquity. It is worth only what the market will bring.

But liquidity, like other measures, can be a matter of degrees. For a crisis account, the one to which a person turns when he or she absolutely has to have cash right now, *Consumer Reports* demands absolute, full liquidity.

THE LIQUIDITY FACTOR

"For an asset to qualify as liquid, it must meet two tests," wrote *Consumer Reports*. "First, you should be able to get your hands on the money almost immediately—at best on the same business day and certainly within a week," explained the magazine. "The second test of liquidity is harder to meet; you must be able to convert an asset into ready cash at a constant, or very nearly constant, value."

While checking accounts, savings accounts, money market funds, and money market checking accounts qualify, stocks and bonds, and mutual funds of these assets certainly would not measure up, since their market value can, and usually does, fluctuate day-to-day.

Some of the best accounts for savers, CDs and Treasuries, fail to meet *Consumer Reports* stringent standards, at least in terms of access. There can be substantial penalties for early withdrawal or for cashing in at the wrong time.

While the *Consumer Reports* standards for emergency accounts apply to short-term savings, *The Super Saver* calls for a declining scale of liquidity, with liquidity growing less important the longer the term of the savings category. That is because, generally, a higher yield is offered by financial institutions as a trade-off for loss of liquidity. CDs and Treasuries, which usually are bought for their superior yields and safety, are not appropriate for contingency uses. And that is fair. Not all savings accounts need to be as fully liquid as money that a person may need for emergencies.

CHASING YIELD

Searching out the best yield can lead a saver on a merry chase, but when other important considerations are ignored, the pursuit can lure consumers into dark and dangerous quarters. In fact, some perfectly respectable and time-honored paths to capital preservation have become overgrown with problems that may escape the notice of a saver whose eye is fixed on yield. Corporate bonds are an example.

CORPORATE COP-OUT

Corporate bonds, a traditional repository of funds for conservative Americans—the legendary coupon-clippers—have lost their appeal for savers.

Bonds of blue chip companies, in the past, have been considered a fitting product for conservative money managers, but the status of the corporate bond has been cast in doubt as a result of the wave of massive takeovers in the 1980s.

The financing techniques utilized in some of the takeovers severely weakened the quality of credit ratings of the corporations, devaluing bonds held by some of the most conservative banks, insurance companies, and bond funds. In addition, the bond market became awash with "high-yield" issues, a euphemism for junk bonds.

TAKEOVER TERRORISM

"Whether individuals buy short- or long-term issues, they should stick with government securities and shun corporate issues, investment professionals say," wrote columnist Anise C. Wallace in the *Wall Street Journal* in January of 1989. "They do not believe that the yields on many corporate issues offset the greater amount of risk they carry.

"That is because even though legislation may result from the upcoming government hearings on leveraged buy outs, it is impossible to predict what if anything will come out of Congress. And in the meantime, there is the possibility that any company's outstanding bonds could be devalued by a leveraged buy out bid. Bonds of RJR Nabisco, for instance, fell more than 15 percent after a management-led group first proposed a takeover last fall."

For the foreseeable future, for savers, corporate bonds have been contaminated by excessive risk.

A COMING BOND BOOM

If legislation is enacted, however, that safeguards bonds against the activities of corporate raiders, they may again be worth consideration. The savings dollars of older baby boomers would fuel a bull market for bonds and other fixed-income assets that could last for years. "I think financial assets will continue to beat most real assets," predicted Prudential-Bache economist Edward Yardini. "Thirty-year Treasury bonds should be down to 5 percent within the next five years. High-quality triple-A corporate bonds will probably yield 5.5 percent."

While the interest rate returns may be down then, the face value of bonds bought before the interest rate decline would appreciate dramatically.

CAVEATS

Regardless of the type of saving mechanism chosen, two bits of advice apply: Pay attention to fees and commissions, and keep good records.

147

FEARFUL FEES

High fees and commissions can shave the value of your investments and financial services faster than a boot-camp barber, warns *Money* magazine. For long-term investments such as municipal bond funds, management fees add up year after year. Be a relentlessly cost-conscious consumer when it comes to financial products and services.

KEEPING TRACK

By keeping good records, you will know which of your savings vehicles have performed well for you and which have not. Everybody makes mistakes sometimes, but you can't learn from past mistakes unless you know what they are.

Additionally, recordkeeping will be important to your family in case something happens to you. None of us ever knows what tomorrow will bring, so our families should be able to easily get the information they need to carry on without us if necessary.

Furthermore, you'll need accurate records at tax time.

INVENTORY OF ASSETS

While our list of savings categories in the chapters ahead may seem slim, incorporating as it does only financial institution accounts, government securities, mutual funds, and insurance products—the list is long enough. A saver who is able to master all there is to know about these things will be better equipped some day to move on to the next level of expertise—to graduate to high-quality, low-risk investments.

Calling In an Expert

Sound like time to call in an expert financial planner? While certain aspects of our financial lives almost always benefit from expert guidance, such as preparing taxes and wills, much of the day-to-day, month-to-month, year-to-year planning is best done by the person who has to live with the financial plan—you.

Only you know how much pocket money you need in order to feel at ease; only you know how much risk you're able to tolerate; only you know how modestly you are willing to live now to achieve some future dream.

You should read books and magazines, attend seminars and classes, and use other methods available to you to become better informed. And when that no longer suffices, the only thing to do is turn to an expert.

These guidelines will help:

• For establishing a financial plan, find a planner who charges only a flat fee or an hourly rate.

• Commission-based services are neither illegal nor unethical, but the advisers should be up-front about how they earn their compensation. Salespeople may be a tempted to push a product for which they receive the highest commission.

• Ask for credentials. Your financial planner should be professionally trained and should meet the highest standards of the relevant professional organization. A certified public accountant can help with a financial plan, as can a Certified Financial Planner. The International Association for Financial Planning has a registry of members from which you may find a candidate.

Even when professional help is solicited, you must be prepared to work with your adviser and to give final approval to any action taken. These people are here to help, but never should anyone be given carte blanche over your money.

In the end, you are responsible for your own financial life.

CHAPTER 12

Banks and Other Depository Institutions

"Don't sell cash short. If you propose to use it,
keep your hands on it . . ."

ELIOT JANEWAY, *Prescriptions for Personal Prosperity*

Ogden Nash once wrote a poem entitled "Bankers Are Just Like Anybody Else, Except Richer." Americans traditionally tended to feel intimidated by banks and bankers, given their power to grant or deny the use of money. It was easy to forget that banks need loans from us as well, via the money we store in their vaults.

However, in the last decade, much of the mystique of banking has fallen away. Back when the industry was heavily regulated, banking was easy and handily profitable. But with deregulation of rates, banks have had to get out there and compete like other businesses. And savers have been forced to become both intrepid and vigilant consumers.

THE CHANGING FINANCIAL SCENE

From the 1930s to the late 1970s, financial services in the U.S. were greatly limited by regulatory restraints on savings products and interest rates. Originally checking accounts didn't pay interest, and savings account interest was at a fixed rate—a conservative 3 percent for banks and 3.5 percent at savings and loan associations.

DEREGULATION COMPLICATIONS

Those were the olden days. The process of federal deregulation of financial institutions began in 1979 and continued in phases until 1986. The competition became torrid as banks, thrifts, thrift and loans, and even usually conservative credit unions battled to come up with the most alluring new product to attract consumer savings.

One of the major reasons that depository institutions fought so hard for deregulation is that brokerage firms were stealing customers away by offering better deals on new products, one of which was only a checking account in disguise.

OUTSIDE COMPETITION

"Merrill Lynch promoted a product called the CMA (cash management account), which offered high interest checking with ability to buy stock from the same account," explained Charlotte Wingfield, senior vice president at Imperial Corporation of America. "Regulators had limited banks to paying no more than 5 percent on checking accounts. Merrill was offering the same service with 8 percent interest because they were not regulated."

The CMA hurt the core business of banks and S&Ls, and they tried to fight back. Finding a way to provide a competitive product and conform to the restraints of regulation often became an inventive task for financial institutions.

PLUCKY REACTION

Wingfield, who worked for California First Bank at the time (1982), noticed in reading the bank regulations that technically, banks were limited to paying 5 percent on checking accounts—unless the money resided in an offshore full-service branch.

California First, in fact, was owned by the Bank of Tokyo, which had a full-service branch in Guam. Wingfield developed an interest-paying checking account that took customer dollars in through California branches, then transferred them offshore to the Guam branch overnight. The company then could pay 11 percent to customers. The new product brought Cal First nearly $200 million in deposits in five weeks.

The bank was sued by the Federal Deposit Insurance Corporation, but won the case. Finally, the FDIC rewrote the regulations to eliminate the loophole, but Cal First's product was "grandfathered" by the court because of the large amount of deposits in the product.

DEFYING CUSTOM

Cal First's is only one of the war stories connected with the evolution of deregulated financial products. There are many more, and the innovation of new products continues both through imaginative thinking on the part of management at these financial institutions, and through outside challenges to the traditional ways of doing business.

REGULATORY CORRECTION

Though deregulation of deposit products is complete, further modifications in regulation for financial institutions are on the horizon. President George Bush signed into law sweeping changes early in his administration that virtually guarantee greater homogeneity among deposit institutions.

A QUARTET OF CONTENDERS

The differences among the four fundamental types of depository institutions have become progressively blurry. Still, they do approach the financial world with somewhat different philosophies, and they still can be found in the telephone book yellow pages under their charter names:

- Banks
- Savings and loans
- Loan companies, called "thrift and loans" in some parts of the country
- Credit unions

The services they offer are remarkably similar now. S&Ls, which formerly specialized in real estate lending, now offer car loans and insurance products. Banks, traditionally commercial lenders, have set up departments for buying and selling stocks and bonds. Yet subtle differences do remain.

BANKING ON PRESTIGE

Of the four, banks still have the most genteel image. And they often have the advantage when it comes to convenience, as far as location is concerned. With nearly 15,000 banks and more than 47,000 branches, they are easy to find. Like other financial institutions, they offer demand deposit, time, and hybrid accounts. Like their brethren, many offer access to funds through automated teller machines (ATMs), and a good many provide trust services.

S&Ls, THE SCRAPPY COMPETITION

The savings and loan industry started many years ago as cooperative associations set up to fund housing and construction loans. But they've come a long way from there. There are now more than 3,000 S&Ls in the U.S. with about 25,000 branch offices. Despite a capital crisis in the industry, the majority of those associations operate solidly in the black and are safe repositories for funds.

A potential customer should compare the rates, fees, and services of S&Ls with those of banks on a product-by-product basis. In today's constantly adjusting market, a bank or S&L may offer the best rate on a money market checking account but the least competitive rate on a six-month CD. Usually the institutions price their products according to the type of money they want to attract. Since their need for funds changes from time to time, so do their rates on various accounts.

Some S&Ls have tended to suffer more than banks in the same economically depressed regions because, based on traditional practices, their fortunes ride so heavily with the tides of the construction industry. For that reason, rates in recession pockets such as Texas had been set exceptionally high by some institutions in an attempt to attract funds to keep the institutions afloat. The once-famous "Texas premium" was popular with savers, but it alarmed regulators, who knew that taxpayers would eventually pay the cost of those rates when the institutions offering them needed federal bail-out.

Yet rates have also been competitive in high-growth areas, such as some northeast and middle-Atlantic states, where most of the S&Ls are quite healthy. This is because the "building societies," as they once were called, need to attract new money, much of it from outside their own region, to fund loans for new construction.

DESERVING OF CREDIT UNIONS

The tiny tots on the block, in years past, were the credit unions. But as deregulation has forced banks and S&Ls to attach fees to basic services and to work harder to attract commercial customers and more affluent private clients, the ordinary checking and saving account customer has turned more and more to credit unions.

More than 57 million people now belong to about 16,000 credit unions from coast to coast. Credit unions can be established by groups of people who have a common bond, such as working for the same employer, engaging in the same profession, or living in the same neighborhood. There are feminist credit unions, church credit unions, teachers credit unions, and some not-at-all-small associations for members of the various branches of the military. In recent years, a credit union's members have had less and less in common, but still, the organization works much like a cooperative.

Convenience often is an advantage, since a credit union can be located at the work place. Also, members have the opportunity to participate in the management of credit unions by serving on the board of directors. An individual can influence policy.

Credit unions frequently operate with low overhead costs, and their profits can be returned to members, in the form of either lower rate loans, higher-rate deposit accounts, more services, or direct dividends.

LAST-RESORT LENDERS

Thrift and loans also have recently worked at transforming their own image. Their principal function is to deal with high risk borrowers. Additionally, they make consolidation loans for consumers who have overextended themselves but can't get help elsewhere. Often known as loan companies, they developed a slightly distasteful reputation by charging excessively high rates on loans for people with questionable or unestablished credit records. Conversely, they paid high rates to depositors. Many were covered by state insurance, but this was often of small comfort in cases where the company became insolvent.

However, in the late 1980s, Federal Deposit Insurance Corporation rules were changed and many loan companies became eligible for FDIC coverage, putting their safety, as far as savers are concerned, on a par with that of banks. Though there are fewer thrift and loans than banks, and their branches aren't always as elegant, they have at times offered some of the best IRA and CD rates around.

CASH MANAGEMENT MANIA

What about the headaches brokerage accounts have given depository institutions with their highly competitive rates on cash management accounts? Often their accounts are offered only to customers with high net worth and sometimes $20,000 or more in cash and securities, and by their very nature are designed primarily for investors, not for savers.

The brokerages may be covered by insurance as well. The Securities Investor Protection Corporation covers customer accounts up to $500,000, with a $100,000 limit on cash. Some brokers purchase additional insurance, boosting coverage to more than $1 million. The coverage, it should be noted, is for broker insolvency only, not market losses on investments.

WILL GOVERNMENT ABANDON DEPOSITORS?

Speaking of deposit insurance, probably no subject has frightened savers more in recent years than the possibility that their banks could fail or that federally insured accounts may be cut loose to fend for themselves in the realm of risk.

It is highly unlikely that the government ever will stop insuring deposit accounts. One of the factors that have built the amazing financial base of this nation and attracted foreign investors in massive proportions is the fact that there were many opportunities to protect money with the considerable economic clout of the U.S. government.

CHECKING CREDENTIALS

For this reason, savers should make sure that any financial institution with which they do business is federally insured.

While that insurance is as trustworthy as ever, changes are occurring, and will probably continue, in the method by which the federal government insures deposits.

That important sign at the institution's entrance should mention the Federal Deposit Insurance Corporation, or one of its two subsidiaries, the Bank Insurance Fund (BIF) or the Savings Association Insurance Fund (SAIF). Credit unions are insured by a smaller, but very stable insurance fund, The National Credit Union Share Insurance Fund.

FDIC PREDOMINATES

Until the 1980s, the FDIC had primarily insured commercial banks, with the Federal Savings and Loan Insurance Corporation (FSLIC) generally covering S&Ls. However, under certain state charters, S&Ls, or savings banks as they are called in some regions, could qualify for FDIC insurance. Thrift and loans were originally covered by state insurance funds, but now in some cases, those with sufficient net worth and other safety requirements also sought and were granted FDIC coverage.

The swarm of failing banks and S&Ls in the second half of the 1980s—by the end of 1988 nearly 500 of the nation's thrifts were insolvent—put pressure on both insurance funds, and eventually, the FSLIC reserve funds were brought down to dangerously low levels after covering a rash of supervised closures of troubled associations.

The adversity in the financial industry could be attributed to a variety of causes, including bursts of inflation and the burst oil bubble in Texas and other southern and western states, permissive supervision of deregulation by federal regulators, willy-nilly granting of bank and S&L charters, and finally, blatant fraud on the parts of some S&L management.

President Bush signed legislation that restructured S&L insurance and instituted other reforms. Now, both banks and S&L insurance is handled by the FDIC.

HOW FEDERAL INSURANCE FUNCTIONS

For depositors, the end result was the same. Deposits are backed by "the full faith and credit" of the U.S. government up to $100,000. When institutions fail, depositors receive their funds within hours of closing, with the loss of interest for only a few days at the most.

MULTIPLE ACCOUNTS

The fact that insurance covers only deposits up to $100,000 has not meant that $100,000 is all you can safely keep in one bank, S&L, or thrift and loan. You can have accounts covered for more than the minimum if the "capacity" and the "rights" on the accounts are vested differently. That insurance, for a couple, could be stretched to as high as $500,000. For example, the couple could deposit $100,000 in each of the following five accounts at the same financial institution:

- An account in the husband's own name
- An account in the wife's own name
- A husband-wife joint account
- An account in the husband's name, in trust for the wife
- An account in the wife's name, in trust for the husband

While the couple could also open insured accounts in trust for their children and grandchildren at that same financial institution, thereby increasing their coverage even further, they cannot extend the limit by opening more joint accounts (with different partners) at the same bank. All ownership in joint accounts is viewed as one at the same institution.

The rules concerning the vesting of accounts may be reviewed by the Federal Deposit Insurance Corporation, and though some experts do not expect the rules to change, consumers should make certain they are following current guidelines.

IRAS ON THEIR OWN

Individual Retirement Accounts are treated separately, however. You are permitted to have an insured IRA at an institution where you already have an insured deposit of $100,000.

TESTING FOR STRENGTH

To achieve additional peace of mind, savers may want to learn something about the financial health of the institutions with which they are dealing.

Many factors can contribute to a bank's dependability. Among them are its longevity, its track record, and its reserves for loan losses versus its portfolio of potentially bad loans.

A key indicator is the bank's capital-to-asset ratio. Using the financial reports that banks usually hand out quite willingly, anyone can establish the ratio by following these steps:

- Determine the bank's capital, also known as net worth.
- Find out the company's total assets.
- Calculate the value of the capital-to-asset ratio by dividing the company's total assets by its capital.

Stronger institutions generally are identified by capital-to-asset ratios of 4 percent or more. A ratio of 3 percent or less could spell trouble.

ASK AN EXPERT

If these numbers seem too difficult to decipher, you can obtain an analysis of your bank's condition from Veribanc, a firm specializing in bank information for consumers. For a reasonable sum, Veribanc will send you a short financial report on any bank or S&L. To make the bottom line easier to understand, Veribanc color-codes its reports. Green paper means a bank is sound; yellow indicates some weakness; pink means trouble.

If a financial institution is federally insured, some people overlook the pink rating. Nervous Nellies, however, should go for the green.

Despite the bleak publicity in recent years concerning financial institutions, this nation still has one of the strongest and most respected banking and brokerage systems in the world. Some experts in financial planning, in fact, say that consumers would be better off going to banks, S&Ls, and similar institutions for their overall financial planning than they would be using financial planning firms or independent practitioners.

These well-established institutions are convenient and relatively trusted, and they offer affordable services.

CHAPTER 13

Finding the Right
Deposit Account

*"If we open a quarrel between the past and the present,
we shall find that we have lost the future."*

WINSTON CHURCHILL

Some people fondly remember the days when you could get a toaster by opening a savings account—an account that paid, at the most, maybe 5.5 percent. You didn't need to know much to use either the toaster or the services of the bank; the accounts were simple to understand.

THE TELLER'S NOW A SALES REPRESENTATIVE

Gone are the placid, boring days; in their place are the brightly smiling men and women who sit at a polished desk in the lobby of a bank and explain the details of dozens of newfangled and sometimes flamboyant savings accounts. These attractive, pleasant people don't look like a high-pressure sales force, but they are, in truth, salespeople.

It's guerilla warfare on Bank Street, and these are the front-line warriors. And more and more frequently, their salary is at least partially based on a commission. The more you deposit, and the more advantageous the account (to the bank) that you select, the more money they earn.

THE CHOICES ARE YOURS

This may sound terrible, but the sales structure is not entirely bad. It means you have to think harder about what you're doing, be more selective, and stand up a little more for what you want and need. But you're also likely to find accounts that are better suited to your personal requirements.

Essentially, there are two kinds of deposit accounts at financial institutions: demand deposit accounts and time deposits.

While a time deposit carries the obligation to keep money in the account for a certain length of time, a demand deposit is available for use at any moment.

THE CONVENIENCE FACTOR

Many demand deposit accounts also are called "transaction" accounts, because consumers without prior notice can make direct or automatic deposits, write checks, and withdraw funds through an automated teller machine, by computer, or by telephone—or in some other way deposit and withdraw on the account.

Demand deposit accounts include checking, NOW, money market, what credit unions call share-draft accounts, and simple savings accounts.

Some require no minimum deposit amounts and impose no fee. Fees and interest rates on certain other accounts vary, and at times, the fees are linked to deposit levels in CDs and other accounts. At the very least, you are guaranteed the return of the money you have deposited (less any fees for services). Some demand deposit accounts also pay an excellent rate of interest.

NOW ACCOUNTS

Interest-earning checking accounts, sometimes called NOW (Negotiable Order of Withdrawal) accounts, are the simplest way to keep your money working and to have it available at the same time. However, most of the accounts have a collection of conditions and caveats, making them both difficult to compare and, sometimes, tough for those on a tight budget to use.

But shopping for the right account for short-term or household cash needs is worth the effort. Don't assume big banks have the best deals. The smaller banks sometimes offer the most flexible conditions with higher rates. Also, by participating in a national automated teller machine system, they can offer accessibility equal to the larger institutions.

The key to handling a NOW or similar account, however, is the minimum monthly balance. Be sure you understand exactly what balance you need, and when, to avoid triggering a fee. If that level of funding is not maintained in the account, you could lose to charges what you had gained in interest earnings. Credit unions sometimes offer better deals on interest-bearing share-draft accounts.

MONEY MARKET ACCOUNTS

Probably the most popular demand account for earning a good rate of return is the money market account. The banking industry's answer to the CMA and the extremely well-liked money market mutual fund, it offers some of the convenience of a checking account, but with a better yield.

However, the minimum balance requirement usually is higher, and there probably will be a limit on the number of checks that can be drawn in a single month. A regular checking account, for example, can often be opened with as little an initial deposit as $50. A money market deposit account, however, may require $500 to $1,000 in minimum balances.

You have the security that, as long as the institution you have chosen is a member of one of the federal insurance funds, all money market accounts are insured up to $100,000. Additionally, savers at financial institutions usually get ATM access to their money market accounts, a feature not always offered by brokerages and mutual funds.

Because rates paid on NOW, share-draft and money market accounts usually are comparatively low, these accounts should be used only for very short-term savings, the money to which you need instant access.

MY MONEY'S TIED UP

With the second category of accounts, the time deposit, the saver agrees to let the financial institution use the funds for a set minimum length of time. The longer the funds are committed, the greater the interest rate premium. Likewise, the more money on deposit, the higher the rate. Time deposit can take various forms.

SAVERS CLUBS

One old-fashioned version of a time account is the Christmas Club (or Hanukkah) account, still offered by some banks. It is appealing to people just learning to save, because they can begin with small amounts and establish the habit of making regular deposits.

The idea is that the saver agrees in advance to deposit a certain amount each week into an account, usually for a year's time. At the end of the agreed period, the bank, credit union, or whatever, pays out the principal and any interest promised. Often these accounts are advertised in the fall and start just before Christmas and Hanukkah, when people are regretting that they haven't saved more for gifts and parties and resolve to do better next year.

The clubs typically allow deposits of as small as a few dollars per week, with little or no fees involved. But early withdrawals or failure to meet the deposit schedule may result in interest penalties. Unfortunately the accounts traditionally haven't paid much interest, and they don't allow much flexibility in increasing deposits. Unless a saver needs such discipline in order to save, a money market account of some type is probably preferable. That could be the reason you have not seen many Christmas Club accounts promoted in recent years.

NOT COMPACT DISCS, BUT MUSIC TO THE EARS ANYWAY

The time deposit most savers recognize immediately is the certificate of deposit. With a standard CD, the saver agrees to keep a specific amount of money in an account for a specific length of time.

While there is a secondary or "resale" market for CDs bought through a broker or a brokerage house, brokered CDs occasionally can put some of your principal at risk.

There also exists a risk of losing part of the interest if you cash a CD before it matures. Penalties for early withdrawal range from as little as seven days' interest to as much as six months' interest. A CD can, however, be used as collateral; some banks will let you borrow against a CD at 2 percent or more than its rate.

CUSTOMIZED AND CROSSBRED

Demand deposits and time accounts are only the starting place. Banks have been changing the ground rules on some accounts, creating variations on others. Dozens of hybrid accounts have appeared, and more bells, whistles, and strings of lights are likely to be added in the future.

In the new deregulated competitive environment, financial institutions must be positioned to make money at any interest rate, pointed out Imperial Corporation's Charlotte

Wingfield, which means that business lines and products must appeal to a diverse audience.

Financial institutions spend months conducting marketing studies and testing new ideas. New products that come on the market "may be hot for several months in a certain market and then fade. In some areas, the product goes on the shelf while in others, it may still have a value to the customers," Wingfield explained.

PLENTY OF PRIVILEGES

In California, for instance, her company discovered that customers were willing to accept a slightly lower rate (in a healthy interest environment) if they could receive easier access to their funds. It was for this reason that the innovative liquid jumbo CD was introduced. Like a regular CD, the account paid a high rate on deposits of $100,000 or more. But customers could gain access to their funds 24 hours a day through an automated teller machine, and could add deposits at any time in the same way. The product also allowed a customer to reduce the account balance to below $100,000. The S&L in that case simply paid a lower rate on balances under $100,000.

That particular account has been especially appealing to lawyers, real estate agents, and others who earn their income in periodic lump sums. When a big settlement arrives in a law office, most attorneys want it to start earning interest immediately. Likewise, funds may have to be removed at unscheduled times to meet obligations. Access is important.

Needless to say, the account was quickly duplicated and offered by other financial institutions as well.

OTHER VALUABLE VARIATIONS

The twists, turns, and tassels on new accounts are bewildering, but they do offer some interesting alternatives to savers.

Available now are:

- CDs with no early withdrawal penalty after the first seven days
- CDs with variable rates
- Name-your-term CDs in which the customer can choose the maturity date
- "Time open" accounts to which the customer can make additional deposits during the term of the certificate

A tax-deferred CD was offered by Home Federal Savings Bank in Washington, DC, according to the *Wall Street Journal*. No money was credited to this one-year CD until the following year, so that depositors could delay taxes on the interest until the next tax period. The depositor gave up the advantage of compounding, since interest was paid on a simple, annual basis, but a relatively high annual rate was offered. Not for the little guy, that account had a minimum deposit of $20,000.

For those with a sense of humor, there are CDs with rates tied to the performance of the Washington Redskins or to the winner of the Super Bowl, and others tied to stock market indexes.

RE-INTRODUCING RISK

In 1989, the government opened the way for a new generation of hybrid accounts by saying it did not intend to regulate banks that want to link interest rates to a specific commodity price.

"Imagine the future;" wrote Linda Stern, a financial writer for Reuters news service, "Government-insured savings accounts that pay more interest if the price of gold rises or corporate bonds that pay more if the group's oil holdings increase in value or their corn crop is especially strong."

Frightening and intriguing at the same time, isn't it?

A California bank, several years ago, tried a savings account tied to the price of gold, and was ordered by federal regulators to cancel the account. It did involve some risk, but it also promised some protection against rapidly escalating inflation. It worked this way: The principal amount of the account was insured and guaranteed, but the interest earnings would fluctuate, tied to the price of gold. For those who rankle at the idea that their rate is fixed and can't move up with the market, it could hold appeal.

DON'T BE CONFUSED BY THE CROWD

But as usual, with the avalanche of new accounts, some trickery was apt to slip in.

Several thrifts in New York, Florida, and parts of the Midwest have promoted "subordinated capital notes." Unfortunately, the advertising for these accounts played down the fact that they were not covered by federal deposit insurance.

Like CDs, the notes were sold over the counter at the thrift branch offices in denominations of as little as $1,000. The yields were about 3 percentage points higher than Treasury securities, and many paid interest monthly. The notes represented unsecured debt, loans to the S&L that offered them, but as "subordinated" debtors, the holders of the notes would be last in line to be paid except for the shareholders if the S&L were to go belly up.

Many people who bought the notes redeemed them, collected their money, and exited the investment unscathed, but all too many were unaware of the risk they were assuming. The whole idea behind an insured savings vehicle is to minimize risk. Even a free toaster doesn't make up for lost principal on an account a depositor believed was insured.

THE BONUS BEAR BECKONS

Actually, the days of the proverbial free toaster aren't over yet. Some banks, S&Ls, and loan companies still offer incentive gifts to attract new customers. Especially when rate wars heat up, and savers can be dazzled away by offers from competitors, the stuffed animals, fishing tackle boxes, airline tickets, quartz watches, and silver coins make a reappearance.

Perhaps boldest of all was the Bank of Boulder in Colorado, which used hunting rifles to target depositors. The guns were not handed across the counter, incidentally; they were ordered from the manufacturer and shipped to a licensed dealer for delivery to the customer. But glitzy come-on prizes shouldn't determine the type of account you settle on. Stick to the fundamentals. What rate of return and what features are you going to get from the account?

BACK TO BASICS

In choosing an account, the saver should consider how two key factors vary from company to company: rates and fees.

The rate, as we've already learned, is the level of interest you are given to keep your money in a specified account at a specified financial institution. Even the minimum yields on savings accounts have been abolished, so studying rates and shopping for them has become no small endeavor.

IDEAL TERMS

Past chapters covered compounding and other effects of time on money. But one also must be sensitive to the frequency with which accrued interest is credited to an account. If interest on an account is compounded daily, but not credited to an account until, let's say, the end of the quarter, the depositor risks losing interest that has been earned. For example, if $500 is withdrawn from a $5,000 account five days before the end of the quarter, the interest on that $500 can be lost for the entire quarter.

Ideally, interest paid on an account should be:

169

- The highest rate available in the market
- Compounded daily
- Credited up to the day the funds are withdrawn

COUNTING THE COST

Because bankers once relied on the low rate paid to savers to subsidize their operating costs, checking accounts and other services were usually free. Since deregulation, fees generally are assessed to services on the basis of how much they cost the bank to provide, how much of a return on capital the bank needs, and other factors.

Some banks attempt to discourage small accounts (that cost them a disproportionate amount to serve) by levying fees on accounts below a certain size or by charging for more than a certain number of withdrawals each month. Even on interest-bearing checking accounts, savers often must monitor their account balances and the number of transactions completed in a month to assure that they stay within the limits necessary to avoid charges or penalties.

DON'T GET MAULED WHILE SHOPPING

When shopping for accounts, comparing features is essential. As mentioned in the chapter on interest rates, many local newspapers publish a daily or weekly rate chart. While not all the local institutions will be included, the charts at least provide a basis for comparison. Some newspapers occasionally conduct a survey of financial institutions, reporting comparative rates and services. Local consumer organizations frequently do the same, making the detailed results available to consumers for a small charge.

Unfortunately, these charts get outdated quickly in a market that responds to competition, interest rate changes, and other factors. For this and other reasons, when you want to check the most current developments, advertisements of financial products are the best source of "deals."

Ultimately, of course, you will have to contact a financial institution to gain additional details and confirm rates, but it helps to have a base-line of information to start out with.

DICKERING OVER YIELD

Believe it or not, there is one financial marketplace where you, personally, can bargain for the best price—your corner depository institution.

If you have a sizable sum of money, perhaps $10,000 or more, you may be able to negotiate for a rate that isn't posted on the rate board, offered in a brochure, or advertised in the newspaper. Most banks, S&Ls and thrift institutions would like to hold on to the "hot" money, the cash shifted by savers in search of the highest yield.

"We teach our tellers to ask customers why they are withdrawing money," explained one S&L manager, "and if they are going somewhere else for a higher rate, we offer to meet that rate."

She admitted that few clients realized that it was possible to bargain. But, she insisted, "Just ask for the branch manager, and ask if the rate you want is possible. If we can make a profit on it, we'll do it."

IN DIVERSITY THERE IS STRENGTH

While intrepid shoppers may end up with accounts at several different institutions, that's all right. It can be useful to have an established relationship with more than one banker. It may be worthwhile, though, to maintain an ongoing relationship with the best banking institution for your situation. If you are getting a free safe deposit box, or sometimes need loans, or often need the other services of a bank, consider this your home bank. It is worth a great deal to have a bank where people know you, trust you, will vouch for your identity on documents, and so forth.

171

SEARCHING THE NATIONAL MARKET

For consumers willing to do business in some other town or in another state, several newsletters offer comparisons of rates and fees for various accounts, with their information covering a great many banks and S&Ls.

By branching out beyond local sources, investors may be able to find rates that are from 2 percent to 4 percent higher.

Residents of California, for example, would seem to be likely candidates for such branching out. California, for some mysterious reason, has historically paid lower rates on deposits and charged higher rates on loans that other states. This defied the law of supply and demand, since California generally has needed to attract outside money to fund its rapid business and construction growth.

Conversely, in Texas during the late 1980s, the so-called Texas premium for CDs brought millions of dollars flocking there to nearly insolvent banks and S&Ls. These were desperation rates, paid in an attempt to keep sinking ships afloat. Eventually, when the ships went down though, the yield-chasers in those accounts were protected by federal insurance.

Those financial institutions that are covered by the Federal Deposit Insurance Corp. or that come under its Savings Association Insurance Fund or Bank Insurance Fund umbrellas, are required to post notice of such insurance on their buildings and in their advertisements. Usually, the presence of federal deposit insurance is noted on letterhead and in other ways that let the consumer know the status of the financial institution. The absence of the federal insurance emblem should be a red flag.

Savers who for some reason have doubts and wish to make certain their bank or S&L is federal insured can contact the FDIC, either in Washington, D.C. or through regional offices.

BROKERED CDS

Out-of-state CDs are available through stock brokerage houses, which also maintain secondary markets in deposits they offer initially. Oddly enough, savers are likely to do better buying CDs through one of these securities dealers than walking through the front door of the issuer. That is because the issuer—a bank or thrift—was willing to pay a higher rate to get, say, $10 million, through a broker rather than going after the money from individuals, $500 to $1,000 at a time. Those who buy CDs from the brokerage can then benefit from that margin. The brokers do take a commission, but the yield often is still higher than it would be via the direct process.

Merrill Lynch, PaineWebber, Shearson Lehman Hutton and Fidelity Investments are among the more active deposit brokers. There is also a cadre of independent CD brokers fanned out through the country, but before dealing with one, carefully check their background, reputation, longevity and track record.

Interest Rate Monitoring Services

"100 Highest Yields" and "Bank Rate Monitor," North Palm Beach, FL 33408. 1-800-327-7717.

"Money Fund Report," P. O. Box 540, Holliston, MA. Put out by the Donoghue organization, this weekly report compares yields, lists portfolio holdings, etc.

"Rategram," The Bradshaw Financial Group, 253 Channing Way, Suite 13, San Rafael, CA 94903. Bradshaw also offers Rate%Gram Online to computer users through The Source.

CHAPTER 14

Government Securities

"New things are made familiar,
and familiar things are made new."

SAMUEL JOHNSON

Americans love to criticize their own government, and talk about its inefficiency, stupidity, and lack of concern for its citizens. All of those things may be true, of course. But in times of economic crisis, the same citizens can be relied upon to dash for the sanctuary of government securities. Americans have a long and esteemed history of that kind of reaction.

PUT YOUR MONEY IN THE POST OFFICE

It was bank failures in the panic of 1907, wrote the *Wall Street Journal*, that spurred public demand for something safer than banks: government savings accounts.

In 1910, the Postal Savings System was created, similar to European postal savings schemes that immigrants from Europe were accustomed to using. At a time when banks were paying 5 percent to 7 percent, the P.O. paid 2 percent. But savers (especially those with modest saving programs) did go to the post office, licking nine 10-cent savings stamps for each $1 deposited, and slapping them on a card.

Come the 1929 stock market crash and the subsequent bank holidays—postal savings really took off. In 1933 the Post Office had nearly $1.2 billion on deposit, 7.5 times more than it had in 1929. By 1947, Americans held $3.4 billion in postal savings. The practice didn't lose popularity until significantly higher savings rates and greater confidence in the economy led to a decline in deposits. Finally, in 1966 the US Post Office stopped accepting deposits. The practice survives in other countries.

PERENNIALLY POPULAR TREASURIES

It probably came as no surprise to economists, then, that after the precipitous decline in the stock market on October 19, 1987, investors retreated, white flags flapping in the wind, to municipal bonds, Treasury securities, and other government-related issues.

In 1988, the Treasury raised $114 billion in net new money. The total outstanding debt was $2.6 trillion, of which the publicly held, marketable portion was $1.9 trillion. Treasuries are the most widely traded instruments in the world. In 1989 Treasury securities totaling $25 billion to $75 billion were bought and sold per day, and earlier in the decade, when interest rates were at record highs, it was common to see trading days of $100 billion.

TREASURY POPULARITY TO CONTINUE

Some financial analysts believe that as the baby boom generation reaches middle age and concerns over retirement begin to dominate their thinking, new money will go into Treasuries (especially bonds) and municipal bonds, potentially increasing their value because of greater demand.

TUTORIAL ON TREASURIES

While government securities offer many benefits to savers, there is a great deal to know about them.

All of the products in this chapter have two things in common:

- They are issued by the federal government or one of its agencies or affiliates, or by a state government.
- They are fixed-income securities.

WASHINGTON'S WARRANTY

Those securities issued by the U.S. Treasury—bills, notes, and bonds—are considered the safest investments that exist anywhere, because they are backed by the legendary "full faith and credit" of the United States government. The money you lend to the government goes to Washington and is used to keep the country's wheels turning. Unless taxpayers revolt and refuse to send their money to the Internal Revenue Service, and/or the government collapses, you'll get your money back with interest.

Most securities issued by agencies or quasi-governmental agencies—the Federal National Mortgage Association, for instance—have only the implied backing of the government. The guarantee is not specifically stated, but chances are superior that the government will stand behind instruments issued by entities operating under its supervision, control, or influence.

LOCAL BACKING

Municipal bonds are offered by state government and local entities, or their agencies. They carry greater risk, but they are rated by respected credit agencies. Many issues are privately insured or, as is preferred by many bond specialists, backed by letters of credit by major international banks.

THE PRICE OF SAFETY

The trade-off for the greater reliability of government issues, of course, is that rates may be lower than bonds or other securities offered by the corporate world. Not always, though. In 1989, savers were able to capture these income producing securities at a 2 percent to 3 percent annual return after taxes and inflation, a return that compare favorably to many corporate issues.

"Throughout most of this century," wrote *Money* magazine, "only chancier investments have provided such a bountiful payoff."

PREDICTABLE INCOME

Given that these are fixed-income securities, you know in advance what your return will be. Though there are many varieties of fixed-income securities, they each, essentially, do the same thing for a saver. They are loans at a fixed rate of interest from the holder of the security to the issuer. The issuer promises to repay the loan in full on the maturity date.

THE BEHAVIOR OF BONDS

Some government securities, such as Treasury Notes and Bonds, trade on an open, secondary market. But you may not be able to buy or sell them at the price at which they were issued or purchased.

This is because face value and rates on the resale market move in opposite directions:

- When current interest rates go up, previously issued fixed-income securities decline in price.
- When interest rates go down, they rise in price.

When rates move higher, a buyer of a security can do better buying a new issue than an old one. Say, for example,

177

you buy a five-year, $1,000 T-Note with a 7 percent yield and decide to sell it two years later when rates have risen to 9 percent. A purchaser has no incentive to pay $1,000 for the note, even though it will be worth that price at maturity. After all, a buyer can get a new T-Note with the same maturity for $1,000 and reap a full 9 percent return. Furthermore, some of the interest on your note has already been paid out. So, this buyer will want to pay less for your T-Note.

Conversely, if rates had declined by 2 percent during the same period, your note would have enhanced value, because the best rate available on a similar instrument would be 5 percent.

TWO WAYS TO PAY SAVERS

Government securities, from T-Bills to zeros, can be broken down into two broad classes according to the method used to compensate investors:

- Coupon securities
- Discount instruments

Coupon securities pay a set rate of interest throughout their lives. Treasury Notes and Bonds and federal agency bonds fit in this niche.

Discount instruments, on the other hand, don't actually pay interest. They are issued at a price lower than their face value. Savers earn a return as the security slowly rises in price until it reaches the face value amount at maturity. T-Bills, U.S. savings bonds, and zero-coupon bonds belong to this camp.

CALL PROTECTION

No small part of the safety and attraction of Treasuries is the fact that they can't be called, or paid off by the issuer prior to maturity. This can happen with corporate or municipal bonds, especially when interest rates fall. The issuers want to wipe out the debt at the higher rate and refinance at a lower rate. This compels the securities holders to find another spot for their money, most likely forcing them to accept a lower level of income than what the called bond offered.

The primary Treasury issues are:

- Treasury Bills
- Treasury Notes
- Treasury Bonds
- Zero-coupon bonds
- U.S. savings bonds

TREASURY BILLS

T-Bills, the darlings of the retirement set and institutional investors, have the shortest maturities of all. Because of their quick maturity, they serve as parking places for short-term money and are part of the "money market." New three-month and six-month T-Bills are auctioned every Monday, while new one-year bills are sold once a month.

With a minimum price of $10,000, T-Bills are sold in increasing $5,000 increments, with a maximum price of $1 million.

The government pays interest on T-Bills at maturity after first selling them at a discount from face value. When the bill does come due, the full face value is paid. The difference between the two prices creates the profit for the T-Bill purchaser.

Treasury Bills are exceedingly liquid, or easy to sell, because they're actively traded in the secondary market. Due to the bills' relatively short maturities, interest rates ordinarily don't fluctuate during the instruments' lifetime, making their price less volatile. During an uncertain economy or highly inflationary times, however, they too have been subjected to the risks of all bonds in secondary markets.

TREASURY NOTES

T-Notes are the benchmark intermediate-term instruments. They are sold at periodic auctions, and are useful for those who wish to lock in higher rates.

They are usually sold in denominations as low as $1,000, though notes with a maturity of under four years may carry a minimum denomination of $5,000. Additionally, they come in denominations of $10,000, $100,000 and $1 million.

T-Notes come in maturities of two, three, four, five, seven, and ten years.

Treasury Notes are coupon securities, and they pay interest twice a year.

There is a secondary market, but the marketability of T-Notes is affected by their longer maturity, which allows interest rates to fluctuate more and perhaps erode principal. However, if rates are falling, they can be sold at a premium.

TREASURY BONDS

T-Bonds, senior citizens as far as maturity is concerned, are also sold at auction, but not as frequently as T-Bills. Before 1970, when interest rates started fluctuating madly, bonds were the bedrock of a conservative portfolio. They didn't go up like stocks, but they didn't go down either; though bonds were boring, the income was a sure thing. Interest rate instability has changed all that, though they are still safe. A return of principal is guaranteed if the instrument is held to maturity, though in a constantly changing market, rates may be quickly made obsolete.

Treasury Bonds can be purchased for as little as $1,000. Due dates stretch out from 10 to 30 years. T-Bonds also are coupon securities, with interest paid twice a year.

There is an active secondary market, with market risks similar to those of notes. By staggering the maturity of bonds in a portfolio, suggest some financial advisers, an investor can insulate his returns from interest rate savings.

BUYING DIRECTLY FROM THE FED

Treasury Bills, Notes, and Bonds can be bought through a bank or brokerage, which may charge fees as high as $50 per purchase. Money can be saved by purchasing them directly from the Federal Reserve, which levies no charge. This can be accomplished by either mail or telephone, as well as by going in person to a regional Fed branch.

To make a direct purchase, it is necessary to open a Treasury Direct account, and then a cashier's check or certified personal check must be presented for payment. When you are purchasing T-Bills by mail, the check should be for the full face value, then you will receive a check for the difference between that amount and the actual price of the T-Bill.

To receive an application for mail purchase, write to the Bureau of the Public Debt, Division of Customer Services, Washington, DC 20239, or contact your regional office.

Individual investors submit "non-competitive" bids, indicating that they accept the going average rate and yield, set not by the government, but through competitive bidding of large-quantity buyers of Treasury securities.

BUYING FROM A BROKER

If there is a possibility that you will sell a Treasury before its maturity, it may make more sense to buy from a broker and pay the service fee. Those bought directly from the Fed must be converted to transferable form before resale, and some dealers may not want to be bothered.

DEALING WITH RE-INVESTMENT RISK

One problem faced by holders of interest-paying notes and bonds is the re-investment risk. When interest is earned and the saver wants to re-invest the proceeds, it isn't always possible to find interest payments at the same or a higher rate. This makes it almost impossible to lock in long-range profitability of a portfolio.

ZEROING IN

Tigers, lions, cats and STRIPS—all zero coupon instruments based on Treasury Bonds—present a solution to the re-investment problem: There are no actual interest payments so there is nothing to reinvest.

In lieu of periodic interest payments, zero-coupon bonds are sold at a deep discount from face value. As an example, a zero-coupon bond that will be worth $10,000 in 1997 was selling for $4,500 in mid 1988.

While it is possible to invest as little as $50 in a zero, with terms ranging from six months to 30 years, most brokers do not want to deal in bonds of that small a size. A minimum purchase is closer to $2,000, with some dealers unwilling to place orders of under $5,000.

To create zeros, Treasury Bonds have been stripped of their coupons by the brokerage firms selling them, thereby separating the interest payments from the principal payments. What is purchased, technically, is a voucher representing claims on the future interest payments at a sharp discount. The original securities are held in trust by a custodian bank, which will pay the entire interest in one lump sum at maturity.

Zeros with feline names are created by brokerage houses, while STRIPS (Separate Trading of Interest and Principal of Securities) are zeros issued by the Treasury itself.

TAX LIABILITY

Even though there are no interest payments on zeros, taxes still must be paid on the interest earned each year. This makes them wonderfully convenient for placement into an IRA or some other tax-sheltered retirement account.

Zeros are also helpful for education funds. While the IRS would tax your child each year as if he or she had received the interest, the interest earnings may not exceed the limits of the "kiddie tax" liability. Under the 1987 tax law change, a child's unearned income of over $1,000 may be taxed at the parents' rate. If an 18-year bond is purchased when a child is born, for example, the interest will accrue slowly in the early years, much of it insignificant until after the youngster reaches 14 years of age. By then, the child is free of the kiddie tax treatment.

TAX EXEMPTIONS

Like other Treasuries, zeros are exempt from state and local taxation, and they are bought and sold on a secondary market.

Zeros have the advantage of locking in high rates when interest rates decline, but present a disadvantage in a rising rate environment. Their rate is stuck at a lower level, and there aren't even any interest payments to invest at higher rates as they come along.

Initially zeros were derived from existing U.S. Treasury Bonds, though zeros now are available for both corporate and municipal bonds.

Corporate zeros are not recommended for savers, because they carry the same elevated risk related to corporate bonds. "What zeros do best is help people finance long-term objectives with a high degree of predictability," noted *Personal Investor* magazine, "and many individuals buy them for that reason alone." They are excellent planning tools for retirement, education funds, or people who simply don't like to spend a lot of time finding a new source for an instrument that has matured.

One last warning. Zeros must be bought from brokers, and there may be hidden mark-ups on the price. This can cause the price—and hence the yield—to vary greatly. Shop around.

BONDS FOR THE LITTLE GUY GROW UP

Though mortgage-backed securities often have hillbilly names like Ginnie Mae, Fannie Mae, and Freddie Mac, it is savings bonds that have had the country bumpkin reputation. For a while, nobody but suckers for patriotism—and those who could save only small portions at a time—would invest in them. But several years ago, that image began to change.

First of all, the Treasury modernized the way interest was paid on savings bonds. Then in 1989, some other advantages were tacked on to lend greater appeal to younger savers.

DOUBLE E'S AND DOUBLE H'S

There are two categories of savings bonds, Series EE and Series HH. Series HH bonds are available only in exchange for EE bonds or similar Treasury securities. They cannot be purchased for cash alone. Series HH bonds provide a regular cash interest payment of 7.5 percent twice a year until a ten-year maturity, at which time the principal is returned to the holder.

By acquiring HH bonds, you can delay reporting the accumulated interest from EE bonds, and hence postpone paying the tax on them for as long as ten years.

SAVING AND SERVING UNCLE SAM

The most popular category, the Series EE bonds, are issued in denominations of $50, $75, $100, $200, $500, $1,000,

$2,500, $5,000, and $10,000. They are backed by the full faith and credit of the federal government.

About 47,000 employers will deduct $10 or more from paychecks at regular intervals for employees' investment in Series EE bonds, and bonds also can be purchased at most banks. There is no sales commission.

They can also be redeemed, on the spot, at the same locations. Redemption tables outlining rates and values are available, usually from the issuer.

MONEY MARKET INTEREST RATES

EE bonds, which replace the old E bonds, pay a variable rate yielding 85 percent of the average return on five-year marketable Treasury securities if held for five years, or a minimum rate, whichever is more. Interest is compounded semiannually.

For bonds issued from November 1, 1982, through October 1986, the guaranteed minimum return is 7.5 percent. For those bought on or after November 1, 1986, the minimum rate is 6 percent. If the bonds are not redeemed at maturity, they go into an automatic extension period, paying the variable rate, until the final maturity date 40 years from the date of issue.

COLLEGE CACHE

Changes were made in the tax law early in 1989 allowing families to use U.S. Series EE savings bonds as a tax-free means of saving for educational expenses. To qualify for the special tax treatment the bonds must be bought after December 31, 1989, and must be purchased by parents 24 years or older. They cannot be placed in the name of a child or other dependent, nor can they have been purchased by grandparents or anyone else.

When the bonds are cashed in, the accumulated interest will be tax-free if the entire proceeds are dedicated to tuition or fees at eligible institutions for the bond owner, or for a spouse or dependent.

Series EE bonds can be registered directly in the child's name. But do take note that, if the bonds are in the child's name, that child can cash them when old enough to write his or her name and to understand what's going on.

The education tax-free benefit is indexed starting in 1990, so salary ranges may change. But in the beginning it is fully available only to single filers with incomes under $40,000 or couples with incomes of less than $60,000. It is gradually phased out for modified income in the $60,000 to $90,000 range on joint returns, or $40,000 to $55,000 for single returns. The savings bond college option is not available to parents with incomes over these maximum amounts.

Savings Bond Tips

• For Series EE bonds, interest is received on the first day of every month for the first 18 months. So, don't cash in bonds in the middle of the month, or you will miss out on about two weeks' interest.

• No matter when the bond is purchased, interest is credited from the first day of that month. So, buy bonds at the end of the month and get most of the month's interest free.

• Lost a U.S. savings bond? The Bureau of Public Debt may be able to issue a replacement, if you can furnish enough information to help locate a record of its having being issued to you.

First, write to the bureau at Parkersburg, WV 26106–1328, and ask for a copy of form PD 1048. On the form, make sure you supply your Social Security number, the serial number of the bond, the date it was issued, and the denomination. If you don't have that information, check with the payroll department or

institution that issued the bond. They may have the data.
 • You can get current rates and information by call-ing 800-US-BONDS, or USA-8888 in the Washington, DC area.

U.S. savings bonds are non-negotiable instruments; they can't be sold on the secondary market at all. If you need the money, the only alternative is to cash them in early.

Interest earned on all of the Treasuries, zeros, and U.S. savings bonds avoid state and local taxes. That makes them ideal for persons in high-tax states such as California, New York, and Massachusetts.

U.S. AGENCY SECURITIES

Securities issued by federal agencies—and many agencies issue them—have a slightly higher risk than those issued by the Treasury itself, since they generally carry only "a moral obligation," or an implicit government guarantee. For that reason, rates usually are higher on Ginnie Maes, Fannie Maes, and their kissing cousins than on Treasuries. Just like Treasury issues, however, some agency securities are exempt from state and local taxes.

Minimum purchase requirements vary, starting from $1,000, and all agency securities must be bought through a broker. Most brokers can offer a list of what is available and the details of the offering.

MORTGAGE-BACKED SECURITIES

Probably best known among the agency securities are Gin-nie Maes, offered by the Government National Mortgage Association; Fannie Maes, issued by the Federal National Mortgage Association; and Freddie Mac participation cer-tificates, issued by the Federal Home Loan Mortgage Corporation. Though each of these instruments operates under separate rules, they are similar.

GINNIE MAE

In actuality, Ginnie Mae does not issue securities. As a part of the Department of Housing and Urban Development, it insures pools of FHA and VA mortgages assembled by mortgage bankers and other lenders. If a mortgage holder in the pool fails to make a monthly payment of principal and interest, the agency will make good if the issuer of the security does not. Since the mortgages in the pool are backed by the federal government, and the pool is insured by the government as well, a Ginnie Mae is doubly secure against default.

However, since Ginnie Maes start out at $25,000 a pop and go up from there, they may be out of reach for small savers. Those interested in their higher interest rates generally would have to buy into a mutual fund, though that has drawbacks as well.

FANNIE AND FREDDIE

Like Ginnie Maes, Freddie Mac participation certificates and Fannie Mae securities are based on pooled mortgages. Though they are not guaranteed in exactly the same way as Ginnie Maes, the instruments of these congressionally chartered corporations carry similar market risks.

There are no additional sales fees for mortgage-backed securities. The cost is built into the price. As bond specialist Marilyn Cohen warns, a purchaser can't know what the actual yield on a mortgage-backed security is until it matures, so some uncertainty does exist in figuring return. A thorough investigation of the instrument and the details of its terms should be made before one is purchased.

GINNIE MAE AND MORTGAGE-BACKED SECURITY FUNDS

Mutual funds, even those offering government securities, are not insured, though overall they have had a long and sound record of survival. But that doesn't mean a government agency security or a fund made of up these instruments isn't without market risk.

Like bonds, their market value declines as interest rates rise. Therefore you would expect the value of these securities to be enhanced as the mortgage rate goes down; it isn't. In an environment of falling rates, mortgage holders hurry out to refinance and pay off the old, costlier mortgages. Investors get their money back, but their high returns go up in smoke.

In fact, with individual Ginnie Maes or funds, the investor gets a little of his or her principal back each month, along with interest earned. While maximum maturity of a pool of mortgages is generally as long as 30 years, the actual expected life of the pool is 12 years or less.

Because the net asset value and the interest income on the funds can both go down at the same time, savers should avoid participating in funds of government securities.

COLLATERALIZED MORTGAGE OBLIGATIONS

Even further down the line in government securities are CMOs (collateralized mortgage obligations) and REMICs (real estate mortgage investment conduits).

While some CMOs can be packaged by Freddie Mac, quite often they are assembled and sold by brokerages or other non-government institutions that do not insure the instrument itself. They are collateralized by government agency securities, but the CMO or REMIC itself does not offer the same guarantees.

The pool has been structured to give a more even cash flow and give a clearer idea of maturity than the direct securities allow. Some of these instruments have offered exceptional returns, though investors often are not told of the higher risk. One CMO packager in Arizona went into bankruptcy in 1989, to the surprise of many investors. Also to their surprise, many other CMO real estate investment trusts (REITS) fell below their offering price in response to that incident, and to rising short-term interest rates.

The CMO REIT, says *Money* magazine, is one of the most complicated instruments in finance, and one of the riskiest. They are not recommended for those who must preserve capital.

MUNIFICENT MUNI BONDS

One of the last legitimate tax shelters, municipal bonds have been increasing in popularity in recent years, so much so, in fact, that demand has pushed the price of bonds higher. "The insatiable appetite for munis by individuals (in 1988)," wrote James E. Lebherz in the *Washington Post*, "helped the tax-exempts outperform taxables. This was true even though the volume of new municipal underwritings was slightly higher, at $103 billion versus $98 billion in 1987."

The higher the tax bracket of the saver, the better munis are likely to look.

"Long-term tax-exempt bonds are the most rewarding of all safe income investment if your tax rate is 28 percent or, better yet, 33 percent," noted *Money* magazine in late 1988.

Nevertheless, municipal bonds must not be confused with risk-free government bonds. Careful attention must be paid to ratings, and on certain municipal bonds, private insurance is available.

TAX REFORM'S IMPACT ON MUNIS

The Tax Reform Act of 1986 made income from certain private-activity municipal bonds subject to the Alternative

Figure 14–1   **Taxable Yields vs. Tax-Exempt Yields**

Maturity	U.S. Treasury Yields %	U.S. Treasury After Tax Yield 28%	33%	Cal. Tax-Exempt Yields %	Taxable Equivalent Yields Federal + Cal. income tax 34.7%	39.23%
6 mos.	8.75	6.30	5.86	5.90	9.04	9.71
1 year	9.01	6.48	6.04	6.00	9.19	9.87
2	9.10	6.55	6.10	6.10	9.34	10.04
3	9.12	6.57	6.11	6.15	.42	10.12
4	9.09	6.54	6.09	6.20	9.50	10.20
5	9.07	6.53	6.07	6.30	9.65	10.37
10	9.01	6.48	6.04	6.75	10.34	11.11
15	9.00	6.48	6.03	7.15	10.95	11.77
20	8.97	6.46	6.01	7.30	11.18	12.01

Source: California Municipal Bond Advisor

Minimum Tax. As a result, new issues of this type of municipal must offer a higher interest rate to compete with the fully tax-exempt bonds.

MORE THAN ONE WAY TO BUY

There are three ways to buy muni bonds:

- Individual municipal bonds
- Municipal bond funds
- Municipal bond unit investment trusts

Individual municipal bonds have a fixed yield and a fixed maturity date, and distributions are paid semiannually. If you buy a $5,000 bond, it will pay $5,000 when it matures, even though the price of the bond may fluctuate if you were to sell before maturity.There is an active secondary market in municipal bonds, but like other bonds, prices move in the opposite direction of rates.

G.O. BONDS OR REVENUE BONDS?

General obligation bonds are issued to raise capital for road, buildings, or other construction and are backed by the taxing authority of the government entity by which they are issued. Revenue bonds, on the other hand, are paid from the earnings of a revenue-producing enterprise such as water, sewer, or electric systems, bridges, or airports, and for that reason some savers prefer G.O. bonds. Both are safe however if only the highest quality ratings are acquired.

Tips for Buying Municipal Bonds

- It's generally best to buy munis issued by the state in which you live. Frequently, that will make earnings exempt from state as well as federal tax.
- Buying individual bonds is the least costly way to invest in munis. With minimum denominations of $5,000 or more, it takes at least $30,000 to diversify adequately.
- Individual investors should limit themselves to top-rated municipal bonds only, since the additional interest on lower-rated (and riskier) bonds seldom is enough to merit the gamble. Rating services such as Standard & Poor's and Moody's provide investors with quality ratings.
- Insured bonds and bond funds can be purchased, but the yield is cut by about one-quarter of a percentage point. Bond insurance has grown in popularity as investors have become more safety-conscious. At the beginning of 1989, about 27 percent of all municipal bonds were insured.
- Look for new issues that can't be called for at least ten years.

MUNI BOND FUNDS

Municipal bond funds often are used by investors with smaller amounts of money to invest, who are able to achieve diversification only in this way. Also, the funds provide monthly income.

However, the mutual fund shares are bought and sold at a net asset value price, which can fluctuate day to day. When you exit the fund, the share price may be more or less than the one at which you entered. Also, the return on the fund floats, in relation to interest rates. Some of the benefits of a muni bond, such as predictable income and a guaranteed exit price, are lost with a muni bond fund.

Since these funds do not protect principal, they are not recommended for savers. Mutual funds are discussed further in the next chapter.

UNIT INVESTMENT TRUSTS

Muni bond unit investment trusts, on the other hand, are recommended by many financial advisors because they offer safety, greater predictability, plus the opportunity for compounding earnings. If you don't need to live off your interest, you can re-invest the interest in any number of vehicles, thereby compounding earnings.

UITs own a diversified portfolio of bonds and pay monthly, quarterly or semiannual interest to the investor. Unlike mutual funds, management buys a set number of bonds and holds them to maturity. It does not reinvest the money that is paid when a bond matures, but rather returns the money to investors.

Often, the minimum investment in a unit trust is only $1,000. They are sold through brokerages or bond companies. The trust can include an up-front sales charge of 4 percent to 6 percent. If the investment is held to maturity, however, the effect of the fee on the return will be minimized.

DON'T BUY MUNIS FOR GROWTH

Even though municipal bonds, like any investment, can have an exceptionally good year, Marilyn Cohen, co-founder and principal of Capital Insight, Inc., a Beverly Hills retail brokerage, summarized the function of the municipal bond market: "If you are an investor looking for the brass ring," she wrote in Jay Goldinger's *Early Warning Wire*, "the municipal bond market will leave you waiting. Remember, the municipal bond market offers safety, security and simplicity."

CHAPTER 15

Mutual Funds

"Money is like an arm or a leg—use it or lose it."

HENRY FORD

The concept behind mutual funds isn't new. In the 19th century, British and Scottish investment trusts were managing the pooled funds of many people with similar investment objectives.

The first mutual fund in this country was established in 1924 by Massachusetts Investors Trust. After the Great Depression and problems with abusive practices in the mutual fund industry, the Investment Company Act of 1940 was passed. The industry really took off after that, and now many hundreds of mutual funds, widely different in nature, are operating in the U.S.

ONLY ONE TYPE OF FUND MEETS SAVERS' NEEDS

The types of mutual funds are legion. They may specialize in stocks that produce income through dividends, in growth stocks with little or no dividend yield, in junk bonds, or in high-grade corporate debt instruments, among numerous others.

Many mutual funds have impressive records, but only one category of account—the money market fund—meets the primary requirement of a saver—an account in which a return of the original investment is virtually guaranteed.

PROTECTED PRINCIPAL

Money market funds trade at a constant $1 price, so that you can exit the fund at the same price at which you bought in. Your shares in the fund are always worth the same amount. Only the interest earnings move with the interest rate market.

HISTORY OF THE MONEY FUND

Unlike the standard mutual fund, money market funds, which the *Wall Street Journal* ranked among the ten most innovative financial ideas, are something of a newcomer to the investment world.

It all started in 1969, when Bruce Bent had a bright idea. He'd been investing premiums for an insurance company, seeking the greatest and safest returns. While rates on certificates of deposit, commercial paper, and other short-term investments were high at the time, Bent and a partner, Henry B. R. Brown, realized that only big players, such as institutional investors, could afford the best six-figure instruments.

"Then inspiration struck:" said *Changing Times*, in a profile of Bent. "Why not a mutual fund? But instead of trading stocks, their fund would trade in . . . money. Investors with as little as $1,000 could get in on the action. What's more, Brown and Bent would stagger maturities so that the fund would be liquid enough to pay off shareholders on demand. The icing on the cake was the form those withdrawals would take: Shareholders could simply write a check. Bent was creating a floating-rate, interest-bearing checking account."

A revolutionary idea, perhaps, but Bent was three years older and $250,000 in debt before the idea really caught fire. The *New York Times* ran an article about the fund he'd established, and within a year, the Reserve Fund, as he called it, held $100 million in deposits.

MONEY MARKET MUTUAL FUNDS FULFILL A NEED

Since then his idea has been cloned so often that total assets in money market funds far exceed those of all other mutual funds combined. By the first quarter of 1989, there were 524 money funds with more than $338 billion under management.

ADVANTAGES

Like other mutual funds, both taxable and tax-free money market funds offer investors several advantages. These include:

- Diversification. By purchasing a large number of different types of issues and maturity dates, the fund is protected against the possible default of any one issue, as well as against abrupt interest rate changes.
- Professional management. The fund managers work full-time at following the economy, interest rate trends and other factors that go into making astute investment decisions.
- Liquidity. A single instrument should be held to maturity to maximize the return of interest and principal. For instance, it isn't possible to cash in only a portion of a T-Note to meet an emergency. A money market fund, however, offers access to all or part of an account at any time by either selling the shares of an account

or simply writing a check. The majority of funds specify a minimum check amount, typically $100, $250, or $500.

- Freedom from excessive paperwork and recordkeeping. Most mutual funds send shareholders monthly statements, and usually this is the only paperwork necessary.

A FAST-PACED MONEY MART

What is the money market? Where does such a fund invest the money of its participants?

Governments, as well as financial and industrial companies, often borrow large sums for a very short time, from overnight to no more than one year. The process of buying, selling, and trading short-term instruments is called the money market.

QUICK TURNOVER

Even though money market maturities can extend for 12 months, regulators require that money funds limit the average maturity of their portfolios to 60 days or less. Frequently, the average maturity is as brief as 31 days. The short maturity of these investments guards against the risk that when interest rates change, the fund is committed for any significant length of time to a lower-than-market rate. Additionally, loans purchased by the funds are more likely to be repaid because of their short maturity.

TREASURIES TO REPOS

Among the instruments bought by money funds are Treasury Bills and federal agency securities; commercial paper issued by major corporations; bankers' acceptances, mostly used to finance foreign trade; bank and savings and loan certificates of deposit; and repurchase agreements involving government securities.

DISTRIBUTIONS

The interest earned on the investments made by the fund are distributed to savers as dividends. Most money funds credit dividends to accounts every business day, but distribute dividends only on a monthly basis. The earnings on the fund can either be taken in cash or reinvested as additional shares of the fund. By reinvesting, the yield is allowed to compound, and thus the account can grow more quickly.

YIELDS

Because the Securities and Exchange Commission requires that all money market mutual funds calculate their yields in the same way, comparison shopping is simplified.

Yields on money funds do change from day to day, and the current yield can be checked in most daily newspapers.

The typical current rates for money market funds can be determined by checking the Donoghue seven-day average rate of the nation's leading money market funds. Most business publications carry it, or perhaps they offer their own index of money rates.

The yields from investments do vary from fund to fund, but not by much. So a saver should select a fund by comparing the following features:

- Management fees and costs, staying away from funds that carry more than six-tenths of a percentage point in annual expenses
- Services offered, such as the ability to write checks and make electronic funds transfers
- How easy it is to buy and sell shares

Figure 15-1   **Ten Big Money-Market Funds**

TEN BIG MONEY MARKET FUNDS

FUND NAME	MINIMUM INITIAL INVESTMENT	MINIMUM CHECK SIZE	PHONE
Cash Equivalent Fund Money Market Portfolio	$1,000	$250	800–621–1148
Dean Witter/Sears Liquid Asset	5,000	500	800–221–2685
Dreyfus Liquid Assets	2,500	500	800–645–6561
Fidelity Cash Reserves	1,000	500	800–544–6666
Kemper Money Market Fund	1,000	500	800–621–1148
Merrill Lynch CMA Money Fund	20,000	no minimum check	609–282–2800
Merrill Lynch Ready Assets Trust	5,000	500	609–282–2800
Prudential–Bache Moneymart Assets	1,000	500	800–225–1852
Shearson Lehman Hutton Daily Dividend	2,500	no check writing	212–321–7155
Vanguard Money Market Reserves Prime Portfolio	1,000	250	800–662–7447

Source: IBC/ Donoghue's Money Fund Report, Box 6640, Holliston,MA 01746

Figure 15-2   **Average Annual Yields of Money Market Funds**

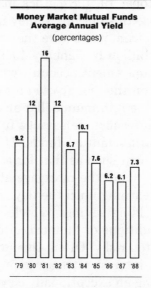

Money Market Mutual Funds
Average Annual Yield
(percentages)

Source: Investment Company Institute, *1989 Mutual Fund Fact Book* (Washington, DC) reprinted with permission

LOAD, NO; FEES, YES

One of the nice features of money funds is that they are "no load," meaning that though management and other fees are imposed, the funds levy no sales charge. Management fees do vary, however, from one fund to another.

Most funds can be opened through the mail. They also can be purchased from branch offices of the investment company, or from full-service or discount stock brokerages.

STRATEGIES FOR USING MONEY MARKET FUNDS

The Washington-based mutual fund trade organization, the Investment Company Institute, suggests that money market funds can be of use to savers in four main ways:

- As a parking place between financial transactions, while you ponder which long-term saving route to take. After the October 19, 1987, stock market crash, many investors chose this option. Money mutual funds grew by $40 billion from just before the crash to an all-time high of $287 billion by January 1989.
- As a cash management account, where you can earn market rates on the money used for ordinary bill-paying. Because the minimum dollar amount for checks is fairly steep, intermediate savings funds are best kept in money market mutual funds. However, if a large monthly payment such as that for a mortgage is made from a money fund, the mortgage allotment will keep working and earning until the day the check clears.
- As a high-yielding savings vehicle when, because of economic conditions or financial circumstances, other options look too risky. Often, this uncertainty is most intense when interest rates are rising, or have peaked and are holding an exceptionally elevated level. Money markets then are suitable even for longer-term savings accounts.
- As a source of tax-free income, when money is placed in a tax-exempt money market fund, also known as a short-term municipal bond fund.

FUND SAFETY

While money market funds are strictly regulated by the SEC and have a superior record of safety, they are not insured by government agencies. The instruments in the funds—T-Bills or Notes, government agency issues, or municipal bonds—may very well be insured. But the fund itself, operated by a private or public company, is not.

The funds, it is important to remember, guarantee no specific rate of return. If a rate must be known for planning purposes, or if a high yield can and should be locked in because of falling interest rates, a money fund is not the place to be.

Savers can intensify the safety of their money market holdings even more by selecting those funds with the majority (or even all) of their holdings in government securities. To ensure maximum security, money fund portfolios should be studied to be sure they invest in the debt products of only the most stable banks, S&Ls, and corporations.

Also, a saver can seek safety through diversification—having funds deposited in several different money market funds.

FIVE VARIETIES OF FUNDS

In descending order of safety, the major funds are:

- Insured funds. Several mutual fund houses have designed the equivalent of a federally insured fund. For a minimum deposit, usually $1,000, they open a money market deposit account for you at a federally insured institution, at which they have negotiated a fairly high rate of return. Each depositor's account is kept separately, so it is insured up to the $100,000 limit.
- U.S. Treasury funds. These funds buy only Treasury Bills. Not only is there practically no chance of default, but also the yield often is exempt from state and local taxes.
- U.S. government agency funds. There is a little more risk, and probably a higher yield, in funds that invest in bonds and notes of federal agencies, those with the implicit, but not explicit, backing of the government.
- Diversified taxable funds. Diversified funds may invest in any money market instruments, so usually they chase the highest yield. This means they hold more commercial paper and only a handful of Treasuries. Again, this bumps down safety and boosts the yield.

- Tax-free funds. Primarily municipal bond funds, these funds are best for those in the highest tax brackets. Even so, U.S. investors have more than $60 billion in more than 150 different tax-exempt money funds.

Finding Information on Money Market Funds

Except for the information from Investment Company Institute, some of the books and advisory services listed below are rather expensive. Most, however, can be found in a public library.

Investment Company Institute, P.O. Box 66140, Washington, DC 20035-6140. For $2, this trade organization will send its Guide to Mutual Funds. In addition to 16 pages of explanatory information, the booklet lists more than 2,700 mutual funds.

Mutual Fund Forecaster (advisory service), 3741 N. Federal Hwy., Fort Lauderdale, FL 33306, 305-563-9000.

Standard & Poor's/Lipper Mutual Fund ProFiles, 25 Broadway, New York, NY 10004, 212-248-2525 (reference books)

United Mutual Fund Selector (advisory service) 210 Newbury St., Boston, MA 02116, 617-267-8855

Wiesenberger Investment Companies Service, 210 South St., Boston, MA 02111, 617-423-2020. (This group has four different publications on mutual funds.)

CHAPTER 16

Insurance as a Savings Vehicle

"When you know a thing, to hold that you know it; and when you do not know a thing, to allow that you do not know it—this is knowledge."

CONFUCIUS

Insurance is one of those unfortunate subjects that very often fill people either with dread, anger, or complete submission out of fear. It can be a dreadfully emotional topic.

INSURANCE RESISTANCE

Consumers tend to react to insurance somewhat irrationally for several reasons. First of all, few of us like to think of catastrophe, death, or other unhappy events. "Enough strife arrives on its own; we don't have to lure it into our lives by planning for it," we often senselessly reason.

A COMPLEX SUBJECT

Second, insurance is difficult to understand. There are many different kinds of insurance and thousands of insurance companies, the fees are mysterious, and the contracts are couched in a combination of legal and financial terminology. It isn't easy to compare contracts and feel assured we are getting what we want and need at a competitive price.

And last, while it is clear what function insurance serves as protection against certain future events, insurance's role as a savings vehicle isn't as clear-cut.

INSURANCE CATAPULTED INTO THE LIMELIGHT

Insurance gained considerable status as a savings vehicle after the 1986 Tax Reform Act, when many other shelters were eliminated. Insurance escaped the ax, because Congress saw it as a necessity. It allows individuals to financially protect themselves and their families in old age and death, thus keeping vulnerable individuals off the public dole.

This chapter sorts through some of the confusion, and offers a guide to the complexities of insurance as a method of saving.

SAVER'S INSURANCE

Since this is not a book on insurance but on saving, only limited kinds of policies are discussed. While automobile, homeowners, health, and accident insurance, to name a few, are important financial tools, they are not directly related to saving.

Only annuities and specific types of life insurance play a role in the goal of establishing safe financial reserves. Annuities, which are becoming increasingly popular as more people realize that they may need to supplement their pensions for many years after retirement, are addressed later in the chapter.

First, let's talk about life insurance. There are three fundamental types:

- Term life

- Whole life
- Universal life

All other categories are variations on or combinations of these.

TERM INSURANCE

Term insurance is a simple form of guarantee with no saving or investment component. You pay a specific premium each month, and the insurance company pays your beneficiaries when you die. It is called "term" insurance because coverage is for a specific period of time and a predetermined amount, and will expire unless renewed. Term insurance is inexpensive for young people, but increasingly costly as people grow older and the likelihood of their death becomes greater. While term insurance itself does not include the possibility of saving or sheltering money from taxes, it is sometimes packaged with other investment products so as to create these qualities.

As recently as 1982, term insurance represented 60 percent of all policies. By 1989, that had declined to 40 percent, mostly due to the active marketing of new products by the insurance industry.

WHOLE LIFE

Whole life insurance costs more than term insurance, because it is "permanent" insurance; coverage never expires as long as premiums are paid. The insured party remits the same amount throughout his or her life, spreading the risk, and also the payments, out over time. Premiums are always the same, even though it costs the insurer less to cover the younger person, with the company's costs increasing as the insured person grows older.

The difference reflected in the overpayment of premiums in the early years allows cash to build up in the policy. This cash can be borrowed, or is paid back to the policy holder when the policy is "cashed in." Though the cash built up does earn a modest amount of interest (usually around 4 percent), the policy does not truly qualify as a savings vehicle. The saving function is merely a side-product of a protection mechanism.

COMPETITION FORCES CHANGE

For years, policy holders were encouraged to think of whole life, and the cash buildup with its small interest earnings, as a form of investment. But as savers became more savvy, and as their high-yielding options expanded, people tended to buy term insurance and invest the resultant savings elsewhere.

Insurance companies realized they needed to come up with a better-paying, more flexible account. The result was universal life, which is built around permanent, renewing term insurance and a cash value fund.

UNIVERSAL LIFE

Universal life policies, which are cash value policies combining a death benefit portion and a tax-sheltered saving portion, more and more are being marketed as retirement savings plans. Despite their many incarnations, fancy packaging, and myriad names, all work in essentially the same way. Part of each premium dollar goes toward the death benefit and expenses, and the rest earns interest either at a fixed rate set by the insurer or a variable rate that depends on the return on one fund or on several funds previously selected by the client.

Universal life comes in two forms: standard, in which premiums are paid at regular intervals, or single-premium, in which the entire payment is made at the onset of the policy.

There are several major benefits to universal life:

- Earnings on the cash value of the policy accumulate tax-free.
- In many cases, earnings on the cash value can be borrowed, at low or no interest, and free of taxes.
- When money is borrowed from a policy in retirement, it does not diminish Social Security benefits.
- The policy offers estate protection, in that if the policy holder dies, the beneficiaries will receive the proceeds from the plan's death benefit, tax-free.

A SELECT MARKET

Because of the fees, commissions, and rules attached, universal life policies (including single-premium policies) are:

- Best utilized only by those who need life insurance
- Best viewed as long-term savings vehicles, with a minimum life, generally, of ten years or more
- Appropriate for a retirement savings account, since the IRS allows more liberal withdrawals after age 59½

Unless a purchaser requires the life insurance portion of the account, it may be better to simply take another route for sheltering earnings. Insurance commissions, which are paid up front, and fees, which are paid as the insurance progresses, are sometimes too high to justify the policies as savings accounts alone. It is these "front-loaded" commissions that rule out insurance as a short-term savings option.

UNIVERSAL LIFE COMPARED WITH ITS ALTERNATIVES

Alternately, the funds could be put into an Individual Retirement Account (even if it isn't a deductible IRA), in which earnings accumulate tax-free. But since no more than $2,000 per year can be put in an IRA, individuals with larger amounts to shelter may choose an insurance option.

Another possibility for savers who do not wish to tie their money up for ten years, or until retirement, is to buy tax-free municipal bonds and continually roll over the principal and interest into new bonds as the old ones mature.

Fees and commissions could be less in either case, but particularly so with the IRA.

CUSTOM-TAILORED FEATURES

Often, buyers of universal life insurance can custom-design policies according to how much coverage they want or need, and how much money they would like to save on a tax-sheltered basis.

HOW MUCH DEATH BENEFIT?

How much life insurance is necessary? Consumers sometimes are advised to buy life insurance with a death benefit of five times their annual income.

This traditional rule of thumb was once considered sufficient to allow survivors to get on their feet. According to other experts, in addition to a lump sum to cover burial costs and settle any hospitalization bills not covered by health insurance, a family will need 60 percent to 75 percent of the salary of the lost wage earner in order to maintain their usual standard of living.

But these standard formulas can leave a family with too little coverage, or can mean that an individual pays too much in premiums for insurance that isn't necessary.

A parent with many young children, for example, will need a different amount from that of a couple who have only one teenage child and who themselves are in their middle years. Similarly, those with small house payments, a large savings reserve, or a well-orchestrated investment portfolio will need less money than families with limited resources.

The best technique is to take out pencil and paper, and list the income that would be available to the survivors and the expenses they will have to cover, then decide what short-fall in income the insurance must meet.

DANGER IN A LAPSING POLICY

But there are drawbacks as well. In addition to the warnings issued earlier in this chapter regarding fees and commissions, policy holders must monitor deposits and loans.

When payments on a universal life policy are made monthly, the deposits should be high enough to cover the life insurance premiums. Otherwise, the amount needed for the premium will be withdrawn from the savings portion, eating away at reserves. Insufficient premiums or excessive borrowing can cause a policy to lapse, in which case the death benefit ceases.

If the policy expires, there is the possibility that the IRS will send a shocking tax bill, insisting that any unpaid loans are investment income.

SINGLE-PREMIUM UNIVERSAL LIFE

Furthermore, in the mid 1980s, single-premium life was all the rage with those who wanted to shelter income in a life insurance policy. Low cost or interest-free loans, without tax consequences, made funds available to policy holders at practically any age, and at any time. Unfortunately, Congress grew impatient with what it saw as abuse of the tax-avoidance practice, and attempted to destroy the tax shelter features of single-premium life insurance.

Legislators did succeed in denting the enthusiasm of consumers for single premium by virtually eliminating tax-free loans to policy holders under the age of 59½. But thanks to an endlessly innovative industry, this type of insurance, which allows prepayment of the entire policy, emerged in a new form.

This new single-premium insurance is being marketed as an estate-planning tool for people who want to shift assets and avoid estate taxes, according to *Financial Planning* magazine: "Planners are suggesting qualified clients put $25,000 to $100,000 currently held in certificates of deposit into single-premium life, where the money will grow tax-free," said *Financial Planning* in a 1989 article. "If a client dies in the next few years, the family will be protected. If the client lives, he can borrow money as needed and pay the taxes then rather than every year, as with a CD. If a client waits until the age of 59½ to borrow money, he will avoid the penalty tax. If the money is never needed, the beneficiaries will collect death benefits free of income and estate taxes."

NURSING HOME OPTION

Some of the new single-premium universal life policies offer an interesting wrinkle. If necessary, the insured person can use the policy's death benefit to pay nursing home costs.

Many senior citizens worry about the eventuality of nursing home care, since health insurance to cover this type of care is often inadequate and usually quite costly. Many older people hesitate to buy nursing home insurance, because they may be paying for coverage they will never use. With this type of policy, if nursing home care isn't needed, the premium pays for a settlement that benefits heirs.

Even so, single-premium policies are complex, and fees are higher than standard policies because they require so much planning, structuring, and explanation on the part of insurance companies and their representatives. Some planners suggest that single-premium is most appropriate for those who most likely will not need the money in retirement, but would like to pass on a lot of money, free of taxes, to heirs.

If retirement income needs to be sheltered, an annuity could be the better choice. Annuities have some of the same characteristics.

ANNUITIES

Voltaire once wrote to a friend, "I advise you to go on living solely to enrage those who are paying your annuities. It is the only pleasure I have left."

The French writer, who died in 1778 at the age of 84, was one of those favored people who manage to win the gamble that is inherent in most annuity policies. People who buy annuities are betting that they will live long enough to retrieve the money they have invested, plus interest earnings. If they don't, the insurance company keeps their premium, and comes out ahead.

If they outlive their invested funds, the insurance company loses the wager. It costs the company more to make the annuity payments than the insured person actually has in the account. The insurance companies may lose a few bets here and there, but their actuarial tables are very good. They win enough gambles to make money on most accounts.

THE ANNUITY CONTRACT

An annuity is a contract under which a company invests a client's money (usually $5,000 or more), promising a payout at a later, agreed-upon date. For example, a 45-year-old school principal may purchase an annuity that will start paying him a monthly payment at age 59½ and pay that amount for as long as he lives. Or, he may choose to take a lump-sum payout at that time.

The annuity premium can be made all at one time, or be stretched out in time payments.

The earnings in an annuity are tax-deferred until the time of payout. As with other insurance, the tax deferral can prove rewarding. If $1,000 were invested at 10 percent a year tax-deferred, for example, it would grow to $6,728 in 20 years. The same $1,000, with gains taxed annually at 28 percent, would increase to just $4,105.

Unlike an IRA, there is no cap on the amount that can be invested in an annuity. And unlike a universal life policy, which may charge nominal interest on a loan (around 2 percent), there is no interest charged on the withdrawal of an annuity. However, the IRS charges a 10 percent tax on annuity funds withdrawn before age 59½, in addition to the regular income tax.

Insurance experts caution savers never to put all of their long-term funds into an annuity, as they would be left with no financial flexibility.

FIXED VERSUS VARIABLE RETURN

Many annuities offer a fixed rate of return, but some allow the client a variable return based on investment results, and the option of switching among several mutual funds.

With a fixed annuity, the insurance company agrees to pay a specific amount at the time the policy matures, either in a lump sum or in fixed monthly payments. With a variable policy, the future payment varies with the income earned by the premium.

Savers must remember, when picking a variable annuity, that risk is involved. Variables offer a crack at capital gains, but also a crack at capital losses. When insurance companies invest annuity funds in stocks, bonds, or any other risk-bearing account on behalf of the insured, they are taking the same chances with that money that they would assume outside the annuity.

In choosing a fund for an annuity, *Money* magazine warns that investors should check a portfolio for so-called junk bonds, sometimes called "high-yield" bonds. "If you turn up more than 20 percent junk in the portfolio, consider switching out" (to a different fund), the magazine recommended.

Whereas fixed-rate annuities generally have appealed to the older person, who sees retirement in the near future, variables usually have greater appeal to younger people, who want to maximize their earning potential.

214

Some variable policies offer a money market account as one option, and that probably is the best choice for savers. However, any fixed annuity that guarantees a 12 percent rate of return is probably going to be competitive over many years, even more so than a variable. Seldom is it possible to achieve that level of return consistently, especially on a tax-deferred basis.

FEES

While returns may sound temptingly high, a buyer must watch out for high fees that eat away those earnings, warns Washington, DC-based financial planner Alexandra Armstrong in a *Lear's* magazine interview. "Annuities have built-in origination fees, annual management fees and exit fees," she said. Armstrong suggested buying an annuity contract from a broker, financial planner, or someone else capable of making an objective evaluation of the policy's merits.

BAIL-OUT PROVISIONS

Look for an annuity with a bail-out provision, especially if interest earnings fall below a guaranteed percentage. If interest declines, withdrawal from the account must be done during a certain "window period" each year. Tax consequences can be avoided if the withdrawn amount is re-invested in a new annuity.

PAYOUT PROVISIONS

There are several ways to collect money from an annuity. Probably the following four methods are the most popular:

- Life annuity, which pays a stipulated monthly income for life. There are no death benefits or surrender values.
- Life with ten years certain, which is like a life annuity except that payments are guaranteed for a minimum

of ten years. Payments go to a beneficiary if the insured person dies early.

- Installment refund annuity, which guarantees a life-time income, and additionally provides that should you die before the payout equals the purchase price, payments would be made to your beneficiaries until the entire amount paid in is returned.
- A joint and survivor annuity, which guarantees payments over your lifetime and that of a surviving spouse.

MONTHLY PAYMENTS VERSUS LUMP SUM

Payments can also be accepted in a lump sum, and financial planner Alexandra Armstrong usually recommends that path or, if possible, a periodic withdrawal of funds, rather than annuitizing. This gives a person greater flexibility in reacting to the changing events of life.

Once annuitization begins, there is almost no way of getting out of the contract. If the recipient needs more money, has an emergency, or would prefer to take less income for some reason, it is not possible. "Anyone who annuitizes," claimed an insurance company official who was even more adamant than Armstrong, "is in a bad predicament."

It may make sense to annuitize only part of a payout, taking perhaps half in a lump sum. That allows the security of a monthly payment and the flexibility of having funds at one's fingertips.

Annuities with a death benefit provision to heirs are also available. While this option adds to the cost of the policy, it may provide greater peace of mind for some individuals.

THE PROSPECT FOR TIGHTER INSURANCE LEGISLATION

Congress already has enacted laws that diminish the tax benefits of single-premium insurance, and there always exists the possibility that even tougher laws will be passed, or that standard universal life will be restricted as well.

Traditionally, such modifications in tax laws have not been retroactive. Policies already in force often are "grandfathered" so that they retain most of their original characteristics.

It is a good idea, however, to check on the status of federal or state legislation before purchasing a new policy. Also, some insurance companies offer easy exit clauses, in case laws change and these changes will affect the policy within, for example, two years.

As mentioned earlier, insurance policies are now packaged in hundreds of different ways. Features from one type of policy are wrapped into the characteristics of yet another type of policy, and entirely new benefits are created. Not long ago, one company began offering a real estate pool, attached to an insurance policy, offering tax-deferred yields on commercial property.

CAVEAT EMPTOR

To make matters even more mind-boggling, each company sells its products under its own proprietary name, monikers that frequently offer no clue as to what the policy actually does.

It is a "buyer beware" market, and purchasers are well advised to do considerable research before making a commitment.

SOURCES OF INFORMATION

For more information on life insurance, contact the National Insurance Consumer Organization, 121 N. Payne St., Alexandria, VA 22314. This association produces numerous publications to help consumers interpret the maze of insurance material. One of its publications, *Taking the Bite Out of Insurance,* carries a list of maximum rates recommended for renewable term policies.

For information on how annuity proceeds will be taxed, stop by an Internal Revenue Service office for a free brochure, Publication 575, *Pension and Annuity Income.*

Also, *Barron's,* a weekly financial tabloid, publishes week-to-week values for variable annuities that are tracked by Lipper Analytical Services.

REGULATORS' INDEXES

State insurance regulators, through their organization, The National Association of Insurance Commissioners, have developed two indexes for comparing insurance policies. These are useful for comparing two or more policies of the same type, though they are of no help when comparing term insurance to whole life, or either of those to universal life.

The interest-adjusted "net payment index" represents the cost of insurance per each $1,000 of death benefit. In other words, it measures the cost of a policy held for life.

The "surrender cost index" measures the present cost of a cash value policy, or the cost of maintaining the insurance, if the policy is then surrendered for cash in ten years.

Insurance agents should be able to supply these index numbers on the policies they are offering. In fact, in most states agents are required to offer this data.

PICK A STRONG, REPUTABLE COMPANY

Because most insurance policies are to become of value at some future—and perhaps very distant—date, selecting a solid, reliable insurance company is much more important than selecting practically any other financial institution with which to do business.

Many states have guaranty funds that step in if an insurance company fails, but often these funds have upper limits on how much they will pay.

To make matters worse, at least ten states—Alaska, Arkansas, California, Colorado, Louisiana, New Jersey, Ohio, South Dakota, Tennessee, and Wyoming—and the District of Columbia have no life insurance and health insurance funds at all.

Of all the states, New York has the most stringent and the most respected insurance laws. For this reason, many conservative consumers prefer doing business with insurance companies that are headquartered and have their corporate charter in the Empire State.

Most advisers are satisfied, however, to deal with companies that for the past five to ten years have earned an A+ rating from A. M. Best, an insurance rating service. An insurance agent can tell you a company's rating, or A. M. Best's *Best Insurance Report* can be found in the reference or business sections of most libraries.

CONCLUSION

The low savings rate in the United States has become the topic of a new national debate, and in the years ahead it will probably be pondered even more intensely.

While your savings habits and mine may seem like personal issues to us, they are not things that touch our lives alone.

SAVING IS A NATIONAL ISSUE

How we use our money, preserve it, and encourage it to grow is unavoidably linked to the greater circle of economic events. Our productivity, including the productivity of the money we earn and save, is what gives this nation its vibrant and vital economy.

"To turn new inventions into marketable goods," wrote American Enterprise scholar Michael Novak in 1988, "a store of previously saved financial resources is indispensable. For it costs money to build new factories and to pay laborers for the long periods of research and production that

220

are necessary, before sales can begin to recoup the original investment and to accrue profits.

"Thus," Novak continued, "the habits of a successful population must be future-oriented. Citizens must abstain from consuming all their gains. They must save and invest in the future. They must be inventive and enterprising. Otherwise their society will stop being creative, stagnate and decline."

THE LESS WE SAVE, THE LESS WE EARN

Unfortunately, reported *Changing Times* magazine, the damages as the result of a declining savings rate are already beginning to show. American salaries have stagnated since 1973, and productivity growth has been alarmingly slow in the past two decades. And again, the impact is circular.

"The trouble is," wrote *Changing Times*, "boosting productivity isn't just a matter of working harder at our jobs. It depends mostly on business investing more and governments spending less. An analysis of the problem by Rebuild America, a nonprofit group, calls for government policies that will encourage saving by individuals and investment by business."

So there it is. Our savings, put into banks, savings and loans, municipal bonds, money market funds, and many other financial instruments, represents an investment in the future for all Americans, including our own progeny.

NEXT MONTH, NEXT YEAR, THE NEXT DECADE

But patriotism isn't the only reason to control expenditures, manage cash, and accumulate wealth. Each of us needs to set aside reserves for our own needs, motives, goals and dreams.

How often have you panicked at tax time, scrimped by during the month that automobile insurance came due, or had to skip a vacation because you didn't have enough money? And for parents who hope to send a daughter or son to college, such tax, insurance, and holiday expenses seem nothing more than minor financial obligations.

It once was easier to save for an advanced education. But now, college costs are accelerating, loans are becoming more difficult to find, and more students vie for a limited number of scholarships.

Additionally, the retirement nest egg is shrinking, warns the American Institute of Certified Public Accountants. Job-hopping, layoffs from corporate mergers and downsizing, and a larger part-time labor pool who don't earn any retirement benefits whatsoever are adding to this problem.

"The solution," suggested by the CPAs trade group? "Plan for the future or work forever."

A PHILOSOPHY FOR SAVERS

Those who set out to improve their savings situation need to understand these realities:

- Their savings accounts are those in which no risk is taken with capital. Later, when the desirable and necessary amounts have been accumulated in reserve accounts, individuals may want to launch into investing, a practice in which capital is put at risk but the potential of greater earnings exists.
- Americans must budget for saving from their current income. Saving may involve some limitation of current spending.
- Consumers must organize a saving cache with specific goals in mind, so as to maximize earnings. This requires some planning, self-discipline, learning, and some attention to changing economic conditions.
- And finally, they need to be ready to spend their nest egg in the designated way when the right moment arrives.

A good way to start the saving process is by recognizing that money is an intensely personal, emotional subject. Few of us can have an entirely objective view of a topic that wields so much control over our emotional and physical well-being.

BEWITCHED BY MONEY

"Money bewitches people," wrote Professor Campbell R. McDonnell in his textbook *Economics*. "They fret for it, and they sweat for it. They devise most ingenious ways to get it, and most ingenuous ways to get rid of it. Money is the only commodity that is good for nothing but to be gotten rid of. It will not feed you, clothe you, shelter you, or amuse you unless you spend it or invest it. It imparts value only in the parting. People will do almost anything for money, and money will do almost anything for people. Money is a captivating, circulating, masquerading puzzle."

Hints for Becoming a Super Saver

• Begin by recording all expenditures for one month. Knowing where your money goes will allow better budgeting, and let you identify areas where it is possible to cut back.

• Establish a budget that will help you anticipate expenses, live within your income, and plan for short-term, intermediate, and long-range needs.

• A fundamental goal of successful cash management is to generate funds for emergencies and for known future events—while at the same time meeting day-to-day expenses. Most families need to keep a minimum of one month's to three months' salary in a savings account, money market fund, or some other place where it can be easily reached.

• Borrow only to pay for those items that add significantly to your asset base, such as a house, a car, or education. When it is necessary to borrow, investigate

223

fees, interest rates, and other charges. In time, these charges easily can double the cost of a purchase.

• A key to successful savings is to diversify accounts, and match savings vehicles to specific goals. As savings grow and you become familiar with different types of accounts, including certificates of deposit, money market funds, and retirement and tax-advantaged accounts, you will gain greater confidence and feel more in charge of your financial destiny.

• Meet your tax obligation, but don't pay more than you need to. Taxes can consume one-third or more of your earnings, and deserve serious monitoring.

GOVERNMENT REFORM OF SAVINGS POLICIES

Even the strongest will and best intentions of individuals, whether they be baby boomers or the babies of boomers, may not be enough. The government must participate in the effort to boost the U.S. savings rate.

Our neighbor to the north, Canada, has set an example for government leadership in the realm. "Between 1972 and 1976," wrote David Sylvester in a 1988 *Fortune* magazine essay on savings, "Canada phased in a series of laws allowing individuals to increase their tax-sheltered retirement contributions. Since then the Canadian personal saving rate, which largely mirrored that of the U.S. for the previous quarter century, has risen from an average of 3.3 percent of GNP to 7.6 percent in the early Eighties."

What the United States cries out for is modification of taxation methods to encourage saving rather than to discourage it; incentives such as Individual Retirement Accounts and college savings accounts; tax-sheltered accounts for the purchase of a first home; the continued reduction of overall taxes so that Americans will have more money for saving—these must become the focus of lawmakers if U.S. productivity and prosperity are to flourish.

GLOSSARY

Accrued interest The interest due on a fixed-income security, such as a bond, that must be paid by the buyer of the security to the seller.

Alternative Minimum Tax This is a federal tax provision designed to ensure that all affluent taxpayers remit at least some taxes. The tax is computed under complex IRS rules that add "tax preference items" (such as depreciation on real property, interest on non-governmental municipal bonds and other tax-shelter deductions) to regular taxable income, then subtracting $40,000 for a married couple filing jointly, $30,000 for single head of household or $20,000 for a married person filing separately. About 21 percent of the resulting figure is the amount of tax due.

Annuity A contract in which the annuitant (buyer) pays a sum of money to receive regular payments, either for a fixed period of time or for life. Annuities primarily are offered by insurance companies.

Basis point A term investment professionals use to describe changes in interest rates. One hundred basis points equal 1 percent. An increase from 6 percent to 12 percent would represent 600 basis points.

Bid-ask spread The difference between the price a buyer offers and the price a seller demands for the same security.

Capital In financial circles, capital generally refers to a storehouse of cash or financial assets. It indicates a fundamental sum, rather than income flow, property, or other tangible investments. It can also mean the net sum of savings.

Capital gain A long-term capital gain is a profit from the sale of a capital asset, such as a security, that has been held for over six months. A short-term capital gain is the profit from selling a capital asset in less than six months. At times, capital gains have been subject to special tax treatment.

Capital loss Any loss from the sale of a capital asset. Capital losses sometimes receive special tax treatment.

Certificate of deposit (CD) A short-term debt instrument issued by commercial banks, savings and loan associations, or other financial institutions. Euro CDs are issued by foreign branches of U.S. banks; Yankee CDs are issued by U.S. branches of foreign banks; jumbo CDs require a minimum $100,000 deposit.

Closed-end investment A company or fund that issues a fixed number of shares that usually must be traded in the securities market. These shares are usually bought and sold through brokers.

Commercial paper (CP) Unsecured promissory notes of corporations and various financial institutions, with maturities of up to 270 days. Used as a money market instrument.

Common stock Securities that represent ownership in a corporation. Shares, or stock in public companies, are traded on various stock exchanges.

Compound interest Interest computed on the interest as it accrues as well as on the principal.

Consumer price index (CPI) Compiled by the federal government, a measure of the change in prices for consumer goods and services over time.

Contingent deferred sales load A fee paid by a shareholder when mutual funds shares are sold. The fee usually is reduced for each year the shares are owned.

Convertible security A bond, debenture, or preferred stock that gives the owner the right to exchange the security for common stock or another type of security issued by the same company.

Coupon A promise to pay interest on a bond when due. Coupons at one time were attached to most bonds; people clipped the coupons and sent them in for collection. Now nearly all bonds are registered, with interest checks simply sent to the registered owner of the bond.

Debenture A bond secured by the general credit of a corporation, and not backed up by assets.

Debt instrument Any instrument that represents a loan between a borrow and lender.

Default Failure to pay an obligation—principal and/or interest—when it is due.

Defined benefit plan A corporate pension plan that promises to pay a fixed amount to retired employees, depending on salary history or length of service. Such plans typically pay monthly distributions which are taxable as ordinary income.

Demand deposit An account with a financial institution from which funds can be withdrawn at will. There is no specific term for which the money must be held in the account, and therefore no penalty for early withdrawal.

Discount The amount by which a preferred stock, bond, or other security may sell below its face value.

Discount rate The interest rate the Federal Reserve charges member banks for loans to keep reserves at the required level. Successive hikes in the discount rate imply that interest rates will go up.

Distribution Money withdrawn from a mutual fund, retirement plan, or similar plan.

Dividend A payment to shareholders on either common or preferred stock. It is usually paid quarterly, though a special dividend is a one-time payment.

Dollar cost averaging A technique for investing equal amounts of money at regular intervals no matter in which direction the market is moving. The theory is that the investor's average cost will be lower than if money were invested in larger amounts or irregularly over the same amount of time.

Equity Ownership of an asset or a corporation.

Face value The value that appears on the face of a bond, usually $1,000, to be paid at maturity. The face value may not represent the market value, however. Also called par value.

Federal deposit insurance A guarantee backed by the full faith and credit of the U.S. government. Accounts at banks, savings and loan associations, credit unions, and thrift and loan companies may be covered by one of several federal programs.

Fixed income security A financial instrument with a specific rate of return, often within a specific period of time.

401(k) plan A qualified employee benefit plan in which employee contributions are made on a pre-tax basis. Both employer and employee contributions compound tax-free until withdrawal.

Front-end load A sales charge for buying into a mutual fund that is paid when the fund is bought. Sales charges can run as high as 4.0 to 8.5 percent and legally can be even higher.

Government National Mortgage Association (GNMA) Also known as "Ginnie Mae." A U.S. government agency whose primary function is to buy mortgages or mortgage purchase commitments and to resell them at market prices to other investors. It also designs and issues new mortgage-based securities.

Government security Generally, any instrument of debt issued by the U.S. government or its agencies or instrumentalities.

Grace period A space of time for which payment is temporarily forgiven. For example, there is a brief span of time with most mortgages and insurance policies during which a loan will not be foreclosed upon or a policy cancelled, even through a payment is past due.

High-yield bond Also known as junk bonds, these are high-yield, non-investment-grade bonds. They are generally considered to carry a greater risk of default than more highly rated instruments.

Individual Retirement Account (IRA) A retirement plan that can be set up by anyone who earns employment income. Interest or investment earning on an IRA is tax-deferred, at least until age 59½, or until retirement. The tax-deductibility of annual IRA contributions is limited to taxpayers who meet income guidelines defined in the Tax Reform Act of 1986.

Inflation An economic condition characterized by rising prices for goods and services. An increasing volume of currency in circulation and a decline in the buying power of cash accompany the rising prices.

Interest Periodic payments made by a borrower to the lender of money for the use of the borrowed money. It is a cost of borrowing.

Junk bond *See* high-yield bond.

Keogh plan A tax-qualified retirement plan for self-employed individuals and their employees.

Leverage The use of borrowed money to invest. The effect is to magnify profits or losses and increase the level of risk.

Liquidate To convert an asset to cash.

Liquidity The ability to quickly convert an investment to cash. The more quickly the conversion can be made, the more liquid an investment is.

Market price The price an asset will bring in the open market. When quoted, it is the last reported price at which a security has traded.

Maturity The scheduled date at which a debt is to be paid, or the principal is returned on a debt instrument.

Money market fund A mutual fund that invests in short-term, relatively risk-free money market instruments.

Money market instrument A short-term debt instrument, such as a Treasury Bill, bank certificate of deposit, repurchase agreement, bankers' acceptance, or commercial paper.

Municipal security A debt obligation issued by states, counties, cities, towns, school districts or other municipal agencies. The interest paid on these securities generally is exempt from federal income taxes and from state and local taxes in the state of issuance. Some mutual funds specialize in these securities.

Net asset value per share The total value of a mutual fund's shares. This could include securities, cash, and any accrued earnings, minus any liabilities, divided by the total number of shares. It is the price quoted in newspapers at which an investor can buy into or sell out of a fund.

No-load mutual fund A fund that levies no sales charge for investment, reinvestment of dividends, and/or redemptions.

Open-end investment company An investment company that continuously buys and sells shares.

Par value *See* face value.

Payroll deduction plan An arrangement between an employee and employer whereby the employer is authorized to deduct a specific amount from the employee's paycheck and to forward it to a savings, investment, or other type of account.

Portfolio The total investment holdings of an individual or an investment company.

Preferred stock A class of stock that has prior claim on dividends before common stock shares. Generally, dividends on preferred shares can be postponed, but they cannot be cancelled. If a company is liquidated, preferred shareholders have a prior claim on assets to common shareholders.

Premium The amount at which a bond, unit investment trust, preferred stock, or other security sells above its face value, or at which a closed-end mutual fund sells above its net asset value per share.

Principal The basic amount invested, excluding interest or earnings.

Prospectus The legal document that describes a securities offering or a mutual fund, and offers it for sale. The prospectus usually contains information required by the Securities and Exchange Commission on officers and directors, financial statements objectives, etc.

Proxy Written permission transferring voting rights to someone who will then vote in place of a shareholder.

Qualified retirement plan A private retirement plan that meets the rules and regulations of the Internal Revenue Service. In many cases, contributions to qualified retirement plans are tax-deductible. Earnings on such contributions are tax-sheltered until retirement. IRAs, Keoghs, 401(k) plans, and 403(b) plans are examples of such plans.

Redemption price Also known as liquidating price or dating price. The amount per share that a mutual fund shareholder receives when cashing in shares. The value of the shares depends on the market value of the company's portfolio of securities at the time.

Repurchase agreement (Repo) A transaction in which one party buys securities for cash and a second party simultaneously agrees to buy them back in the future at specified terms.

Rollover Movement of funds from a corporate pension plan to an Individual Retirement Account, or from one IRA to another. The Internal Revenue Service permits only one IRA rollover per year if the investor handles the money. There are no such restrictions on transfers, in which IRA money moves directly between trustees at the investor's instruction.

Round lot   One hundred shares. This is the standard number of shares used to trade stocks. It also is the number of shares to which prevailing broker commission rates apply. The commission is higher on a smaller amount, or odd lot.

Secured   Debt that is backed by assets, of either an individual or a corporation. A corporate bond, for example, usually is secured. A debenture, however, is not; it takes its place in line to be paid behind the bond in case of bankruptcy.

Securities and Exchange Commission (SEC)   An independent agency of the U.S. government that administers the federal securities laws for the protection of shareholders.

Securities Investor Protection Corporation (SIPC)   An insurance plan for a brokerage accounts, backed by federal guarantees. It provides protection for customers' cash and securities that are on deposit with an SIPC member firm, in the event that the firm fails. Protection is limited and usually is supplemented by private insurance bought by the brokerage firm.

Simplified employee pension   A plan that allows larger Individual Retirement Account contributions for employees or self-employed persons than otherwise would be available.

Single-premium variable life (SPVL, or investment life)   Describes an annuity much like single-premium whole life insurance except that the premium is invested in pooled investment funds, rather than in an account similar to a bank certificate of deposit. Some policies offer several choices of mutual fund-like investments.

Single-premium whole life (SPWL, or income life)   Describes an annuity in which, under current law, the single premium is fully invested in a certificate-of-deposit-like instrument, the buildup of cash is tax-free, and death benefits are exempt from federal income taxes.

Tax-deferred income   Income on which the tax is levied when it is distributed.

Tax-exempt fund (tax-free fund)   A mutual fund in which the portfolio consists of securities exempt from federal income tax, usually municipal bonds or money market obligations.

Tax-exempt security   A municipal bond or other debt instrument that is exempt from federal taxes. Some are called triple-exempt, because they are also exempt from state and local taxes. Regulations vary from state to state.

Tax shelter   An investment used for deferring, eliminating, or reducing income taxes.

Total return   A calculation for return on investment that includes both the income derived from an investment and the growth in the asset value. In a stock, for example, it would include the dividend yield plus the increase in share price.

Unit investment trust (UIT)   A type of mutual fund that buys a fixed number of real estate, debt, or fixed-income obligations and sells them to investors in units. The portfolio is not actively managed and is liquidated according to a specific schedule.

Unsecured   Debt that is not secured by assets. A personal loan, versus an auto loan or a home mortgage, generally is unsecured.

Variable annuity   An insurance annuity under which the dollar payments received are not fixed, but rather fluctuate with the market. Most frequently, investors will have a choice of stock, money market, or bond funds.

Variable life insurance   Unlike straight life insurance policies, variable life lets the holder direct some or all of the cash value into the financial markets, usually through mutual funds.

Whole life insurance A traditional form of life insurance, in which purchasers pay a fixed annual premium for a fixed death benefit and a cash value that grows at an interest rate determined by the insurer.

Yield Income earned from an investment, usually expressed as a percentage of market price. Total return includes interest plus capital gains or losses.

Yield curve The relationship between interest rates (or current yield of the security) and the maturity of a security. It is also used to forecast the future direction of interest rates.

SUGGESTED READING

Belth, Joseph M., *Life Insurance A Consumer's Handbook*, Indiana University Press, 1985.

Brownlie, William, *The Life Insurance Buyer's Guide*, McGraw-Hill, 1989.

Gardiner, Robert M., *The Dean Witter Guide to Personal Investing*. New York: New American Library, 1988.

Hallowell, Edward M., MD, and William J. Grace, Jr., *What Are You Worth?* New York: Weidenfeld & Nicolson, 1989.

Klott, Gary, *The New York Times Complete Guide to Personal Investing*. New York: Times Books, 1987.

Loeb, Marshall, *Marshall Loeb's 1989 Money Guide*. Boston: Little, Brown and Company, 1988.

Miller, Theodore J., *Kiplinger's Make Your Money Grow*. Washington, DC: Kiplinger Books, 1988.

Mintz, Joe A., *Consumer's Guide to Compound Interest*. Dallas: NROCA, 1988.

Schnepper, Jeff A. *How to Pay Zero Taxes*. Reading, MA: Addison-Wesley Publishing Co., 1989.

Sherman, Michael, PhD, *Comprehensive Compound Interest Tables, Newly Revised and Updated Edition*. Chicago: Contemporary Books, 1986.

Van Caspel, Venita, *Money Dynamics for the New Economy*. New York: Simon and Schuster, 1986.

Weiss, Geraldine and Janet Lowe, *Dividends Don't Lie: Finding Value in Blue-Chip Stocks*. Chicago: Longman Financial Services, 1989.

INDEX